Deloitte Consulting

Focusing on customers

the role of technology in business

A Euromoney Publication

Focusing on customers:
the role of technology in business

© Euromoney Publications PLC

Published by
Euromoney Publications PLC
Nestor House
Playhouse Yard
London
EC4V 5EX
Tel. +44 (0) 171-779 8888
www.euromoneyplc.com

Director Christopher Brown
Group publisher Roger Davies
Associate publisher and editor Rohan Freeman
Adverting manager Angus Chapman
Advertising sales Debbie Ormonde
Advertising sales Shaun Edwards
Sub-editor Michael Halls
Production editor Norma Ewart
Editorial board Lawrence Hutter, Ian Pattison, Kate Amos, Jane Henderson.
Directors Padraic Fallon (chairman and editor in chief), Sir Patrick Sargeant, Richard Ensor (managing director), CJ Sinclair, Takashi Hosomi, Neil Osbourn, Christopher Brown, Dan Cohen, Gerard Strahan, JP Williams, John Botts, Edoardo Bounous, Richard Jell, Colin Jones.

ISBN: 185564 747 8

The information contained in this publication should not be relied on as professional advice and should not be regarded as substitute for detailed advice on individual cases. No responsibility for any loss occasioned to any person acting or refraining from action as a result of material in this publication is accepted by the editors, authors or publishers. If advice concerning individual problems or other expert assistance is required, the service of a competent professional adviser should be sought. The opinions presented by the individual authors do not necessarily reflect the opinions of Deloitte Consulting.

Wouldn't it be good if you could
Stop the clamour

The clamour of dozens of front office vendors all saying basically the same thing

We save you time and money. We cut your time to market. We increase customer retention. We improve your bottom line. Perhaps they do. But do they integrate seamlessly with your back office? And will they be around to support you in five or ten years time? Can you still hear them? At Oracle, we know a thing or two about integration. And quite a bit about staying power too. So when we talk about a front office solution to partner our strengths in the back office, you can bet on it. You can bet on it to integrate customer relations with your enterprise, from supply chain through to human resources. You can bet on it to lower total cost of ownership and aid faster speed of implementation. And you can bet on Oracle delivering the 360 degree view of the entire business you have always wanted. ORACLE FRONT OFFICE… see further with our vision and don't bet on the competition. To learn more, visit our Web site at *www.oracle.co.uk* today or call +44 (0)1625 544 455.

ORACLE®

Focusing on customers

the role of technology in business

Foreword   **6**

Chapter 1
Business trends   **9**

Chapter 2
Enabling technology trends   **15**

Chapter 3
Call centres   **23**

Chapter 4
E-commerce   **33**

Chapter 5
Customer information management   **45**

Chapter 6
Sales force automation   **55**

Chapter 7
Consumer manufacturing and retailing   **61**

Chapter 8
Financial services   **69**

Chapter 9
Public sector   **77**

Chapter 10
Telecoms   **85**

Chapter 11
Utilities   **89**

Chapter 12
Making it happen   **99**

Biographies   **109**

I know which buttons to push.

{ The ones that give me access to all your confidential files. }

N
e
t
T
o
o
l
s

Dr Solomon's/McAfee
Total Virus Defense

PGP Total Network Security

Sniffer Total Network Visibility

Magic Total Service Desk

SHE'S THREE KEYSTROKES AWAY FROM BRINGING YOUR NETWORK TO ITS KNEES. UNLESS, OF COURSE, YOU'RE PART OF THE 80% OF THE GLOBAL 1000 WHO HAVE CHOSEN NETWORK ASSOCIATES FOR THEIR NETWORK SECURITY AND MANAGEMENT. IF SO, BREATHE EASY. IF NOT, IT'S PROBABLY NOT HER LOOKS GIVING YOU SHORTNESS OF BREATH. TO FIND OUT MORE ABOUT NETWORK PROTECTION, AND A COMPREHENSIVE INFORMATION PACK ON NETWORK ASSOCIATES FAX +44 (0)1753 827434, OR VISIT WWW.NAI.COM. OK, NOW EXHALE.

network
ASSOCIATES
Who's watching your network

Foreword

By Lawrence Hutter, partner, customer dynamics, Deloitte Consulting

The corporate world's greatest challenge has always been attracting new customers and keeping them. Nothing new there. But over the last 10 years, the attention of the world's business leaders has been increasingly directed at responding to the demands of globalization and internal restructuring. As the 90's draw to a close, however, their attention is once again pointing towards their primary objective.

The battleground is the customer's wallet. The protagonists are the world's largest corporations. Their weapons are technologies which increase understanding of individual customers and offer better access to those customers. The victors will be those that can order their entire organization around the challenges of getting cheaper, more profitable and more loyal customers.

The backdrop to this scene is the growing sophistication of consumers themselves. We live in an age of expert buyers. Customers are becoming ever more critical and demanding. They know that they can play the market and are placing higher and higher demands on merchants to give them what they want — and immediately.

Companies now face the challenges of offering products with zero defects, tailored to the needs of individual customers, delivered and sold through a multitude of still evolving channels and cushioned in faultless levels of imaginative customer support and information.

The aim of this book is to begin the process of focusing corporation's efforts on exploiting the opportunities that these new challenges present. The book asks questions about the standard business models readers will need to adopt and the technologies that can help underpin their efforts.

Lastly, I would like to thank all the authors for their efforts in helping to bring all the chapters together. I am indebted to the wealth of their experience and knowledge which has contributed so much value to this book.

Does your right hand know what your left hand is doing?

If not, customers may be slipping through your fingers.

Breakdowns between the customer interactions in the call center and the fulfillment processes on the back end can result in frustrated customers. In fact, 68% of customers leave a company due to poor service. Fortunately, Mosaix's solutions integrate customer-centric processes across your enterprise to help you deliver end-to-end service and hang on to your most valuable assets—your customers.

Introducing ViewStar® 5.0 Call Center Edition, the first of a new generation of Customer Relationship Management (CRM) products from Mosaix. Regardless of how your customers contact you—phone, fax, Internet, or correspondence—our process-driven application framework consistently and reliably manages all channels of interaction and the fulfillment activities they trigger.

With ViewStar 5.0 Call Center Edition, you have complete customer information at your fingertips, when and how you need it, to provide highly personalized service. The result is a powerful competitive advantage: more efficient and effective service, which leads to increased customer loyalty. For the whole story on ViewStar 5.0 Call Center Edition and our CRM product line, go to **www.mosaix.com,** or call **1-888-4MOSAIX.**

The customer crowns himself

Chapter 1: Business trends

Overview

The great boardroom issues of the 1990s — downsizing, streamlining, globalization, total quality and process re-engineering — were largely internal battles of how companies structure themselves. But the issues and battles of the next decade will be external — business leaders will focus outwards and back on the customer.

Out of the whole range of business trends in the recent past, just three stand out:

First, the accelerating pace of technology change and innovation.

Second, the growing competition in mature markets. New, profitable markets are harder to find.

Third, the growing maturity and awareness of the customer. Expectations for service and quality have changed.

Businesses have to change to keep up with these trends. Only a few will be sufficiently innovative to be able to rely on a stream of new must-have products and service. The majority of businesses have to realize that keeping close to customers is a strategy that the combination of process, technology and people must support. The strategic imperative for them is to know:

- which customers wish to purchase;
- which products or services;
- through which channels;
- at what time; and
- and how these demands can be satisfied at an acceptable cost.

At the same time, they must understand how the next customer will be won — and at what cost. This must be counterbalanced by working out which customers will leave next, what the cost is of keeping them and whether it is worth doing so.

Customer focus

The need to stay customer-focused is hardly a new message. The embodiment of customer focus is the small shopkeeper who greets customers by name, knows their buying habits and anticipates their needs. Yet the small shopkeeper and the small business around the world are all losing ground. The new discussion around customer focus is about how to maintain such relationships just as effectively but far more efficiently.

So what is driving the renewed focus on the customer?

Companies:
- are competing for a greater share of the customer's wallet;
- aim to keep growing through customer acquisition and loyalty, and at the same time to reduce the associated marketing and sales costs;
- are instilling among their staff a greater willingness to serve; and,
- are responding to deregulation and privatization, realizing they have lost their monopoly power over the customer.

Customers:
- have greater knowledge and experience of the marketplace;
- are less loyal;
- have an increased understanding of their own worth;

● are placing higher demands — immediate gratification, zero defects and ultimate tailoring; and,

● have a better understanding of what constitutes value.

Who is the customer?

In a business environment, there are two types of customer:

● business or trade customer

● end customer or consumer.

The labels 'business customer' and 'consumer' are convenient but dangerous. When used as general terms, they imply a commonality among customers, which often does not exist. Even with apparently anonymous business customers, there is always a series of faces, of one-to-one relationships behind the organization name.

The 20th century has concentrated on mass production, mass merchandising and mass communication. The result has been to bring a range of goods and services within the reach of a broad range of society. The 21st century will see a change towards greater personalization, and greater recognition of the interests and wishes of the individual.

Thinking of the customer as an individual is difficult in a mass market society. Market segmentation has been the answer up to now, using demographic, socio-economic and behavioural evidence to define clusters of like-minded individuals. Sampling techniques allow some degree of confidence in matching products to target customer groups, but they are, by definition, imprecise.

For example, is the consumer who shops for brand 'X' in supermarket chain 'Y' attracted by the brand proposition or by the retail proposition? The answer is usually a combination of both. The brand and the retail proposition together influence the consumer's shopping experience.

Shopping malls have dominated US shopping for years. In their latest European incarnation, they have a flair and style that puts them firmly into the sightseeing realm. They are no longer simply collections of stores but major attractions in their own right. Shoppers travel long distances to visit and admire. The retail proposition of an individual retailer is reinforced by their presence in the new cathedral. Yet the brands within the stores still exercise power and attraction at close range.

Manufacturers and retailers try hard to understand what motivates shoppers. They have sought to get closer to individual customers through loyalty schemes and the use of consumer databases, to understand what drives individual consumer behaviour. These activities will continue, not just as one-off market research studies but as an in-built way of doing business — being close to the customer.

Aggregating individual behaviour into discernible patterns and continuing to segment customers more carefully will always be important. The use of customer information databases and related analysis tools supports the increasing micro-segmentation.

Specialist TV channels aimed at minority markets have proliferated in the so-called "fragmentation of the media". The new technology-enabled technique known as interactive marketing takes it to its extreme. It allows each customer to take part actively in the marketing process. They themselves select via the kiosk or PC screen those marketing messages that best match their circumstances. Interactive marketing moves the business much closer towards being able to offer a relevant, uniquely tailored offer to the customer.

In the end, the customer is always an individual. The individual performs a number of roles — at home, at work, while on the move. The more that a business knows about individuals, the better placed it is to influence their expectations and respond to their needs. (As an aside, the use of rule-based intelligent

In today's business environment, customer loyalty can never be taken for granted. It must be cultivated and treasured. Traditional market research techniques are still important, but as you move towards the ideal of one-to-one relationships, you need to base decisions on real-world information – information that mostly already exists in your corporate databases and ERP systems such as SAP AG's System R/3.

The SAS Solution for Customer Relationship Management allows you to tap into that information and hear the authentic customer voice. It surfaces valuable information about individual customer preferences, provides a solid basis for customizing products and personalizing messages, and reveals new sources of business based on accurate segmentation and profiling.

The SAS Solution for CRM not only informs you on how best to retain (or win back)

good customers, but also suggests ways to increase lifetime value through up-selling and cross-selling. And it helps you to optimize your operational CRM by providing effective feedback on your campaign activity.

For further details visit us at www.sas.com and check out our CRM pages. Or e-mail us at ckelly@eur.sas.com to request your free information pack on the SAS Solution for CRM.

Your customers are talking to you. Can you hear them?

ABC1 male, single, 25-34, loaded

I'll be your best customer ... in five years

I'll need a loan soon!

Into classical music, drive 10,000 km per year

I bought Brand X... so sell me Brand Y!

Treat me as an individual

Speak to me with one voice

Cut down the waiting time

Target customer... over here

Take me off your list

Talk to me now, or I'll talk to the competition

Hello, is anybody listening out there?

I'm ready to buy now

Dual income, no kids

SAS Institute Inc.
World Headquarters
SAS Campus Drive, Cary, NC 27513 USA
Tel: +1 919 677 8000, Fax: +1 919 677 4444
In Canada call: 1 800 363 8397
Web: www.sas.com

SAS Institute
European Headquarters
P.O. Box 10 53 40
Neuenheimer Landstr. 28-30
D-69043 Heidelberg, Germany
Tel: +49 6221 4160, Fax: +49 6221 474850

The business of better decision making

SAS Institute

agents to search out the best bargain over the Internet could cast doubt on the statement that the customer will always remain human.)

Globalization

A few years ago, emerging multinationals worked on the "Think global, act local" premise. The mantra then changed to become "Think global, plan global and act local". Many large companies became successful in this way. They learned how to balance global vision with local autonomy.

The more that a business knows about individuals, the better placed it is to influence their expectations and respond to their needs

It all worked well as long as the customers remained local. However, times have changed. Many organizations have gone through the multinational stages and emerged as truly global organizations, both as suppliers and as customers. In turn, suppliers that wish to deal with such organizations now have to recognize they have to be able to act global themselves.

1992 was a key year in the commercial integration of Europe. The experts pointed to the massive increase in cross-border trading that would happen as companies spread their wings. Although, the process took some time to get underway, the pace has picked up — a mere seven years later a common European currency has been introduced across 11 independent European states. It took decades for an equivalent German Reichsmark to become established after the German *Zollverein* (customs union) was founded in the 1830s.

Dealing with customers on a global basis requires highly effective technology to assemble and evaluate the mass of data collected locally.

Technology

Even in these days of learning organizations and flattened management hierarchies, the basic control loop — plan, execute, monitor — retains its place at the heart of management practice.

Technology enables these processes, involving:
- fast capture of data from distant operating units;
- communication to a central decision point;
- presentation in a usable format for decision-making; and,
- communication of decisions back out to the far-flung operating units.

Technology, however, creates in the customer's mind as many threats as it does opportunities. The biggest of these is considered to be security. Company's must not only ensure that the electronic channels which they offer their customers are secure, they must ensure that they are seen to be secure. The technology exists but the responsibility for creating confidence in people's minds lies with companies employing those technologies.

Choice

Customers have become more mature in their purchasing habits. From an early age children can distinguish between advertising that informs and advertising that oversells. They learn that the advertising promise may not be matched by reality.

Lifestyle changes also mean that traditional channels may no longer have the force they once had. The gradual decline in some developed countries of television as a popular entertainment means that alternative marketing channels are required to ensure communication with target segments of the population.

Advertising helps put the individual in a position to make a choice. One way in which businesses respond to greater customer expectations for choice is to offer non-traditional sales and distribution channels. Long before the arrival of

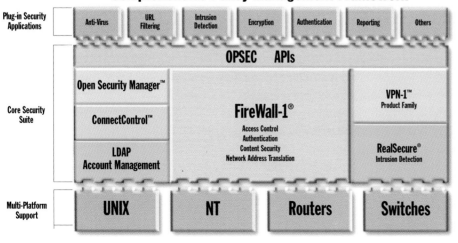

Internet e-commerce, mail-order and telephone shopping were well established in the consumer market. In the business market, paper-based order forms have given way to telephone and EDI.

Pace of change

The accelerating pace of change in late 20th century society has attracted much comment. Alvin Toffler's *Future Shock* in the early 1970s pointed the way to the symbiosis between an impermanent, uncertain existence counterbalanced by stability zones which allowed individuals to retain a sense of their past and their future.

In the commercial world, the pace of change has placed increasing demands on the quality of decision-making. Many organizations are now battling with how to instil a value-based management approach throughout their operations. They want the people in their downsized organizations to use the same criteria in their decision-making as are used in the boardroom.

Decision-making

The area of decision-making has been especially fertile ground for management and technology approaches. 'Information for motivation', 'Management by objectives', 'Decision support systems', 'Executive information systems' and 'Data warehousing' are all fashions that buzz around the honey pot of better decision-making.

While organizations have undoubtedly made great improvements in their decision-making over the last 30 years, the continuing number of bad decisions indicates room for improvement. The area of promotions and campaigns is one such example. Often campaigns are run with little more justification than the fact it was run at the same time last year. The data is simply not there or is not reliable.

Lifestyle changes also mean that traditional channels may no longer have the force they once had

When presented with performance data, the first question asked should be: "Are we doing better or worse than planned?"

The need is to see clearly what is happening in terms of upward or downward trends, and then to investigate and understand the causes. Drilling down to lower levels of detail may uncover what is taking the business forward or what is holding the business back.

This kind of presentation and analysis has serious limitations. It is simply one-dimensional — "are we hitting or missing objectives?" The individual is left to take a decision about how important this particular objective is relative to the rest of the organization's objectives. This is often too complex to even contemplate — let alone to do with any guarantee of success.

The new generation of decision-making involves asking a second question: "Are we getting the balance right?"

Arriving at an answer involves thinking about short and long-term issues, about profit versus growth, about reconciling conflicting objectives. In the past such weighty decisions were a management responsibility. Today the drive is on to make such decisions at an operational level, as close to the customer as possible. Organizations are trying to support their people in making such decisions, empowering them and encouraging them to be innovative and responsive — in line with the organization's overall objectives.

Enterprise transformation

Businesses have found it hard to make a gradual break with the past. Many have needed to use shock treatment to transform their businesses, or have endured shocks such as those IBM experienced in the 1980s. They have restated their core values and strategies. They have instigated programmes to implement the right combination of processes (how to work), information and technology (the toolsets) and organization (people).

Dealing with issues such as customer focus, globalization, new technologies, customer choice, pace of change and decision-making requires businesses to exhibit the following positive characteristics in the processes they perform, the way they organize themselves, and in the technology they use.

Businesses must be:

- Responsive: listening to customers and taking fast, appropriate action;
- Flexible: prepared to change to meet (reasonable) customer expectations;
- Low cost, high service: optimizing the cost/service equation;
- Innovative: showing market leadership in product and service innovation;
- Cross-functional: breaking down old-style departmental boundaries; and
- Informed: working on the basis of visible, accurate and timely information.

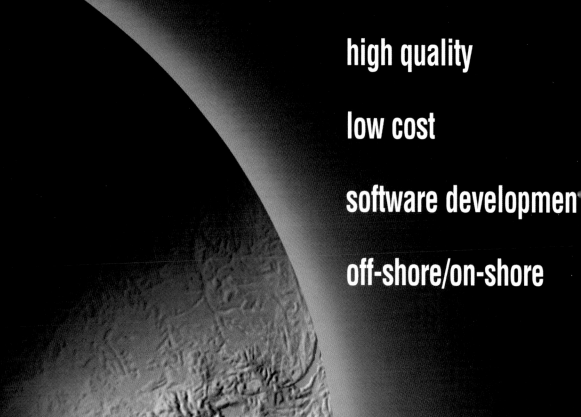

Chapter 2: Enabling technology trends

Overview

For someone who grew up in the age of the typewriter, the invention of correcting fluid was a breakthrough.

It may not have been the most important technological breakthrough of the 1960s, but it benefited millions of people. Many more millions were affected by the introduction of bar code scanning (EPOS — electronic point of sale) in retail outlets, which provided faster and more accurate service to the consumer. Even more people experienced the change from telex to fax within the decade.

A technology trend is made up of hundreds of such events, insignificant on their own, yet combining to redefine the way individuals and businesses communicate with each other. Technology changes that make an immediate and dramatic impact on the individual are few in number. Not surprisingly, some of the most important trends are under the surface. Their shape is discernible only when the evidence is pieced together.

So, for example, over the last decade the telephone has become an ever more powerful tool of business communication. Telephone banking, telephone shopping and telephone access to information are all familiar to the customer.

At the business end, CTI (computer telephony integration) is making the transition from large organizations to smaller sized organizations, allowing more customers to experience better service over the telephone. There is an immediate link between the customer's telephone or identification number and their computer records. The more businesses that use CTI, the more the customer will expect instant recognition when placing a call. Both the customer and the service provider benefit from the improved speed and quality of the interaction.

Similarly too, new analysis tools provide deep insights into consumer preferences and the factors that influence purchasing decisions. They can evaluate much larger amounts of raw data as they seek to match cause and effect.

Businesses are finding new customers via the Internet, as well as protecting relationships with existing customers who want to do business over the Internet.

The use of e-mail, electronic forms and web browser technologies to support individuals in business is growing. Intranets and extranets are beginning to provide the basis for much wider information sharing within and between organizations.

CTI and large customer information databases were pioneered in the mid-1980s. It has taken time for the technology to mature, and for organizations to develop powerful business applications. Internet technology took off rapidly in the mid-1990s and has been a focus of attention ever since.

Each technology trend is allowing businesses and individuals to take actions that were either difficult or impossible only a few years ago. They are enabling a series of business applications that are bringing direct benefit to both businesses and individuals — in terms of revenue, profit, convenience and lifestyle.

What next?

So what comes next? The word being used increasingly is "virtual", as in virtual reality or virtual private networks. Virtualization means enabling large parts of the population to do business outside traditional boundaries and constraints.

The Internet is the initial implementation of this. More discoveries will be made under the heading of virtualization. People will expect to live in both the physical world and in a virtual world that they have moulded themselves.

Discoveries in the other four areas will not stop. The revolution that started 250 years ago is still gathering pace. Continuing the geometric growth of recent years leaves one breathless but there will be no let up in the increasing speed of change.

The lesson from history is that a new technology does two things. It opens up choice, and it may displace an earlier technology. The speed of change is such that many organizations now employ specialist technology-watchers. They try to keep abreast of pioneering technology developments before they hit the headlines, so that the businesses they represent can gain first-mover benefits.

The risk of being a pioneer is to end up in a dead end technology, often after expending considerable cost and effort. The semi-intelligent Smith-Corona typewriters are one such example. At the other end of the spectrum, the laggards risk being overtaken by competitors and losing their livelihoods.

The spectrum is increasing in size. It is possible to enjoy a profitable niche anywhere along the spectrum — as long as it coincides with a set of willing customers.

The table below lists a number of current technologies with an assessment of whether the technology is pioneering, progressive (new but proven) or stable. Stable means that the risks associated with using the technology are well understood. It does not mean that it has stopped developing.

How state-of-the-art are the technologies?		
Area	**Technology Status**	
Home	● home shoppping, virtual reality	Pioneering
		Progressive
	● voice, touch-tone to call centre	Stable
	● touch-tone only	Stable
	● videotext	Stable, old
	● PC via web + plug ins	Progressive
	● PC via web, no plug ins	Progressive
		Pioneering
	● interactive TV	Pioneering
	● web enabled TV	Pioneering
	● home management systems	Pioneering
Retail outlet	● smart cards (loyalty)	Stable
		Progressive
	● kiosk booths	Progressive
	● self scanning check-outs	Stable
	● self edge prices	Stable
		Progressive
	● electronic signage	Progressive
Front office	● CTI (computer telephone integration)	Stable
		Progressive
	● voice recognition	Progressive
		Pioneering
	● customer management systems	Progressive
	● document management	Progressive
	● electronic security; signature, authentication, payment	Progressive
	● ERP (enterprise resource planning) systems	Stable
	● customer/product/stock visibility, optimization	Progressive
Back office	Supply chain management	
	● bar codes Progressive	
		Stable
	● RFID (radio frequency identification) data tags	Pioneering
		Progressive
	● satellite positioning	Progressive
		Stable
	● Analysis planning	
	● data warehousing, data mining	Exist
	● neural networks	Progressive
	● costing systems	Exist
On the move	wireless, satellite	Pioneering,
		Progressive
	portable computing (web access, phone, home managment etc)	Pioneering
		Progressive

The drive homewards

Predictions for the next decade see people spending more time in the privacy of their homes. Teleworking has been a moderate influence in this direction. The wish to be surrounded by personalized creature comforts is a more powerful influence. Technology helps provide these comforts.

As a customer, the individual at home already uses the telephone extensively and is beginning to experiment with the PC. The combination of ordering and receiving deliveries at home is long established, for example, in mail order.

It is intriguing to see how technology is enabling cheaper processing of home orders (ordered via a PC, printed automatically in a warehouse, delivery vehicles routed optimally) and driving a throwback to the pre-refrigeration and pre-car days when groceries were delivered to the home.

Retail outlets

In retail outlets such as banks and shops, technology is being used to encourage frequency of visit (from footfall to getting the customer into the store) and to help the customer once there.

Loyalty cards have become widespread, with smart cards capturing information about shopper behaviour on the card as well as on the large computer at head office. When combined with back office customer information databases and analysis tools, in store offers to the customer can be truly personalized.

It is a return to the old days when the storekeeper knew the buying behaviour of each individual customer and adapted in-store offers accordingly. The convenience of self-scanning checkouts is reserved for priority customers. Shelf edge prices can be changed more rapidly, allowing localization of the offering to match the needs of a particular outlet at a particular time of day.

Front office

Customer-facing front office systems have been through several generations already. Placing an order directly over the telephone instead of via an order form is no longer new. Telesales scripts ensure a degree of consistency and quality in the interaction with the customer. They enable cross-selling, up-selling and configuration to make sure the customer is properly served.

New technologies are aimed at supporting — and occasionally replacing — the human interaction between a business and its customers.

One of these is optimization. Optimization routines are nothing new. The techniques go back to the heyday of operational research in the 1970s and were used in industries such as mining, energy and transport to improve business and service efficiency. The growth in computing power means that these routines are now capable of processing many more variables than their counterparts even 10 years ago.

At the point of entering a sales order, the customer service representative asks the computer to check the impact of taking this order on the rest of the outstanding order book. In a few seconds, the computer recalculates the entire supply chain and makes its recommendation. It mentions any required actions, like asking a supplier to deliver a quantity of raw materials a day earlier. It warns which orders for lower priority customers will fail to be delivered on time.

Back office

The technology in the back office may be out of sight but it is vital for providing customer service. Again, current developments in technology are enabling organizations to be much more sophisticated in knowing and responding to the needs of their customers. Increasing computer power makes it possible to capture and use much larger amounts of customer information than was possible before.

Corporate networks make it possible to access, use and enrich this information in every contact with the customer.

The development of large customer databases has its pitfalls. When used for direct marketing, the crude and inaccurate information held about individuals has rarely resulted in response rates (much less sales conversion rates) of barely 2% of those contacted.

Many organizations have been overwhelmed by the amount of data they have captured and been unable to process. The result has been a series of data dustbins, where the only solution has been to start again. Only a few organizations have reached the point where the technology is supporting them in knowing what adds value to the individual and what does not. The British Airways frequent flyer loyalty programme continually looks for new products and services attractive to its members — who in turn remain loyal.

Speed of response

A defining characteristic of business in the next 10 years will be a focus on speed of response. One way of managing the risk/reward balance better is by being able to respond to events more quickly. This requires the necessary business processes, organization and technologies.

Predicting the success of a consumer promotion is notoriously difficult. What worked last year may not work this year. However, retailers now have models that can tell within the first few hours of trading whether a promotion will exceed or fall short of expectations. Fast communication back to suppliers allows manufacturing to be stepped up or reduced.

The same applies to the use of new technologies. Businesses have to be prepared to step up or reduce their investment. Time is of the essence, which is why staying close to the customer is so important.

Staying close to the customer

Staying close to the customer is something more substantial than making a knee-jerk response to events in the market. It is about having a clear strategy of being close to the customer and doing two things tactically:

● discovering and meeting latent customer wishes for products, services and ways of doing business; and,

● encouraging or nudging the customer in new directions — in other words, demonstrating leadership.

Whichever way it happens, the risk of adopting a new technology is reduced if a business takes its customers with it.

Traditionally, understanding customer requirements has been the role of the market research department. Leading organizations recognize that the responsibility for meeting customer expectations has to be spread more widely across the organization. They look at their internal operations to see what adds value to the customer relationship and what does not. They remove the functional blocks that get in the way of customer focus.

Managing the cost/service equation

Service costs money. One way in which businesses respond to customer demands for different ways of doing business is to increase the number of their sales and distribution channels.

Proliferation of channels is costly for a business to manage and leads to channel conflict. Some businesses respond by limiting their channels to market. In so doing, they consciously limit their target customer base to those segments that they believe will generate maximum profit. Alternatively, they try and divert the low margin customers to the cheaper channels.

Low price airlines cut out the travel agent by requiring consumers to book directly. When the customer waits in a queue to make a telephone booking, punctuated by exhortations every 60 seconds that it is quicker to book via the airline's web site, some customers will inevitably lose interest and use another more convenient channel offered by a competitor.

This may not matter, so long as the call centre systems can record how many callers failed to wait and management can decide whether it is worth investing in more customer service representatives to handle the demand.

The technology enables better management of the cost/service equation. The point is that enabling technologies only work if the business objectives, processes and organization have all been worked out and present a coherent image to the customer.

The pace of technology change means that businesses no longer have the luxury of time to find out what appeals to their customers and what does not.

Knowing what customers want, expect, like and dislike is nowadays too important to be left to the market research department alone. It has to be a key business objective, which informs every aspect of process, organization and use of technology.

Full Spectrum
is the Future for Orange™

MOBILE COMMUNICATIONS GIANT, ORANGE IS COMMITTED TO CONSTANT INNOVATION TO ENSURE CUSTOMERS RECEIVE A LEVEL OF QUALITY SERVICE APPROPRIATE TO ONE OF THE UK'S MOST FAMOUS BRANDS. SIGNIFICANT INVESTMENT OVER THE LAST TWO YEARS HAS ALLOWED ORANGE TO DEVELOP ONE OF EUROPE'S MOST ADVANCED CALL CENTRES.

Orange launched just four years ago, with the aim of shaking up the mobile phone industry by concentrating upon customer needs to offer genuine added-value. A range of innovative services allowed Orange to build a substantial customer base very quickly.

However, the mobile phone operator also knew that customer retention would be a key to profitability in a market renowned for high churn rates. From the beginning, Orange has viewed every contact with the customer as an opportunity to build longterm relationships with its subscriber base. This strategy has been extremely successful. While boasting the lowest churn rate in the industry, Orange are embarking upon an ambitious strategy to double their corporate subscriber base and see complacency as the enemy.

Few companies have had to come to terms with the phenomenal rate of growth already experienced by Orange. Just two years ago, the company had 400,000 subscribers. Today there are over 1.3 million. Perhaps even more remarkable, the Orange call centre operation handles double the number of calls compared to 18 months ago, with very nearly the same number of operators.

The technology which makes this possible is breaking new ground. In 1996, Orange made a major commitment to the evolution of its geographically separate call centre operations. At that time, the systems required constant monitoring in order to divert calls manually between call centres, should one location experience a surge in traffic. This was performed by a dedicated team. Jean-Luc Lorenzi, Principal Engineer, Intelligent Network Systems Design explains: "It was a crude, resource-hungry process, which gave us very little flexibility in terms of balancing call traffic between sites to deal with any overflow at peak periods. We needed a

system to support single call resolution within a virtual call centre. Just as importantly, the right technology would enable us to refocus on management information to improve our understanding of customer needs."

Orange selected Rockwell's Spectrum system after a thorough technical and commercial evaluation, which included a visit to Rockwell's corporate headquarters in the United States. Jean-Luc continues:
"We needed a world-class supplier who offered us an open route to the future and would reliably support Orange's quest for excellence. From the beginning Rockwell were very open about where they were going as a company. There was a productive synergy with the approach adopted by the two companies.

"Spectrum offered a wealth of features which only a couple of other suppliers could match. Rockwell's responsiveness to additional requirements was also a definite asset. They have a 'can do' attitude which is very important to Orange." In addition, Spectrum will, in the future, interface with the Orange telecommunications network, a feature which the mobile operator intends to exploit to full commercial advantage. In fact, Rockwell's open architecture, which includes its Gemini voice processing system, allows Orange to integrate all their IT building blocks across the entire organisation.

Spectrum was implemented within a very short time frame. Rockwell provided staff training, as well as a 'train the trainer' program to ensure a smooth transition. According to Jean-Luc Lorenzi, "There were very few teething problems. The system went in on schedule with no interruption of service and then call centre business went on as usual! In fact, the system

makes life much easier for our call centre employees at all levels."

Orange employs around 1,000 agents at its Darlington call centre and a further 340 in Bristol. Spectrum routes major calls between both sites for mission-critical services such as the Customer Services Helpdesk. It also provides multiple skill queuing, directing each enquiry to the agent group with the most appropriate skill set.

More important than the technology are the people. Orange believes its employees come second only to its customers. Agents are empowered to make all the decisions they need to handle a call, supported by Merlin, an in-house business flow management system and Inference, a problem-solving package. Every item of information is available across the whole business.

The mobile operator is currently using Rockwell's Gemini voice processing system to develop the potential for auto-fulfilment. Jean-Luc explains, "This system was a crucial part of the Rockwell offering, as it allows us to fully leverage CTI and Intelligent Network technology within our call centres. We believe it is an added benefit to provide more intelligent, automated services for straightforward enquiries, provided customers always have the option to talk to a live operator."

The Orange call centre operation will continue to evolve. The company is preparing for the introduction of mobile number portability on 1st January 1999, which offers the greatest opportunity yet to win an even larger share of the market. As Jean-Luc says, "Nothing is ever static at Orange, we are improving all the time." ∎

Exceptional *thinking*
Unlimited VISION.

CONTACT: NIGEL WELSH, ROCKWELL ELECTRONIC COMMERCE LIMITED, EAST WING, GROUND FLOOR, ST MARTINS PLACE, BATH ROAD, SLOUGH, BERKSHIRE SL1 3UG. TEL: 0800 634 0200 FAX: +44 (0) 1753 876702
www.ec.rockwell.com info@ec.rockwell.com

Chapter 3:
Call centres

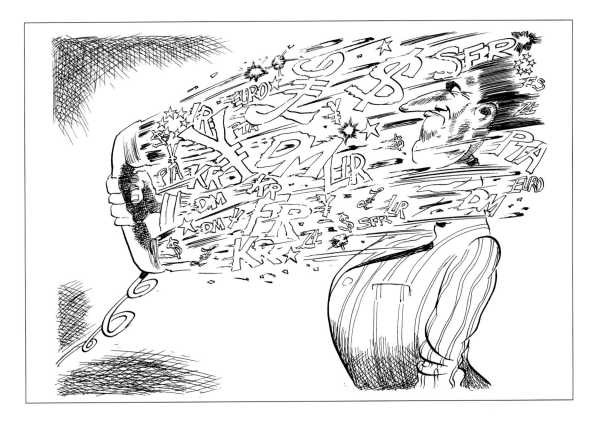

Overview

Call centres are not automatically profitable. There is also the opportunity of lost business. In the example below a call centre lost thousands of dollars in just six minutes. Worse, in the longer term, those same minutes may have lost future business worth tens of thousands of dollars.

Two callers seeking international flights ring the call centre. Caller one, the first in the queue, is looking for the cheapest of short-hop flights. Caller two is a businessman wanting to buy a first class transatlantic ticket. After six minutes of caller one ahead of him, caller two hangs up annoyed. Caller one promises to ring back: possible profit $20. Caller two telephones a rival airline: lost revenue $4,500 and possibly a relationship worth $50,000 a year.

The example above shows how call centres — introduced by many organizations to cut costs — can lose money.

The early adopters of call centre technology won a short-term competitive advantage as their sales and customer service costs fell. However, now that their competitors are catching up, profits are again being squeezed, and the opportunities for cost reduction are fewer.

Whatever the industry, the challenge now is to use the call centre to increase revenues. The key to this is differentiating the low-value customers from the high-value customers — separating the $20 commissions from the $50,000 high rollers. Firms that do not respond to this challenge will be left with the low-revenue, high-cost leftovers. But for those that succeed, the call centre will become a powerful tool for identifying and exploiting high-value customer relationships.

The call centre is not just a commodity — it may hold the key to future profitability.

Call centres

From telephonist to account manager

The call centre phenomenon emerged in the 1970s and 1980s, and is still growing rapidly. The US was the first to embrace the idea of doing business over the telephone. It was followed closely by Europe, which now has the highest growth rate of any region.

Call centres were first established as a lower cost alternative to doing business face-to-face. Early adopters were typically in retail services such as the travel industry, where there was no physical product to change hands. It is easy to see the attraction — why pay commission to a third-party travel agent when the booking could be taken directly over the telephone from the customer?

Other industries were quick to catch on. Retail banks realized that they could slash the cost of account servicing by shifting their customers from branch outlets to call centres. As well as avoiding expensive town centre real estate, staff costs fell dramatically as a result of the improved efficiency of using a large pool of call takers, rather than a small branch team.

Having established a call centre to handle inbound calls from customers, many businesses realized they could exploit the call centre to generate new business. Outbound call centres started to appear, with operators making cold sales calls — telemarketing — or following up written sales enquiries from potential customers.

Combining the two activities, known as blending, produced a very efficient product, with any troughs in in-bound call volumes being filled as operators switched to making outbound calls.

The skills of the telephone operators (often called agents) have changed. From being straightforward call takers, the role has evolved to the extent where many agents are involved in a diverse range of new sales and customer retention activities, as well as straightforward order taking and account servicing.

The role of telephone agents		
Type of activity	**Inbound**	**Outbound**
Sales	• Taking sales calls in response to advertising • Making sales appointments	• Cold calling • Calling in response to written sales enquiries
Customer	• Account servicing (eg retail bank transaction) • Handling complaints • Providing product information • Responding to requests for after sales service • Accepting claims (eg warranty or insurance) • Billing enquiries	• Advising of delivery times • Recovery of outstanding payments • Activating new services (eg a cellular phone)
Customer loyalty		• Special offers • Welcome calls to new customers

Call centre technology

The change from telephonist to account manager has been supported — and in some cases facilitated — by developments in call centre technology. Most call centres employ several basic building blocks.

• **Specially tariffed telephone numbers.** These are often used to encourage or deter calls. A free (usually x800) prefix is often used to attract sales enquiries. Alternatively, a premium rate number may be used to reduce the cost of long calls to a software supplier's technical helpdesk.

• **Automatic call distribution (ACD) equipment.** This is used to route inbound calls to agents. ACDs will also queue calls while waiting for a free agent. Most will support multiple queues, so that calls coming in on a number reserved

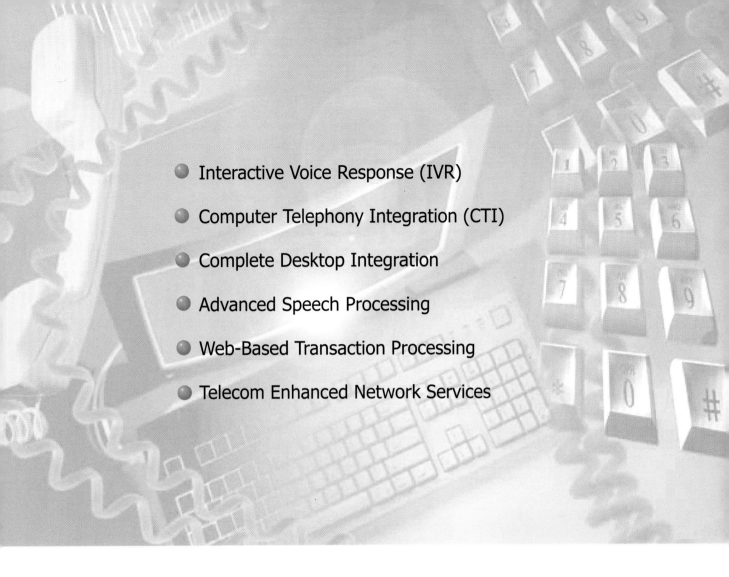

- Interactive Voice Response (IVR)
- Computer Telephony Integration (CTI)
- Complete Desktop Integration
- Advanced Speech Processing
- Web-Based Transaction Processing
- Telecom Enhanced Network Services

Providing You With Best-of-Breed Call Center Technology Solutions...

Are you looking for advanced technologies to maximize your call center? Ways to improve service? Lower costs? And, technologies that give you the best ROI?

Look to Periphonics, who has joined forces with Deloitte & Touche Consulting to bring you the "best-of-breed" technology solutions. For almost 30 years, Periphonics has been setting the benchmark for products and professional services that automate call processing for customers throughout the world. Periphonics customers represent a variety of industries–American Airlines, Charles Schwab, American Express TRS, Internal Revenue Service, The

Hartford, Mellon Bank, Sprint, Entergy and UPS, just to name a few.

Industry experience brings value to your call center. Talk with us about Periphonics' award-winning solutions in CTI, IVR and Advanced Speech Processing technologies that can help your organization communicate with customers easier and more efficiently.

Let us show you how you can maximize your call center. Call us today at 1-800-411-9084 or 516-737-8566 for a FREE Consultation. Or, visit us at the Deloitte Solutions Center of the Americas.

Periphonics

www.peri.com

USA • Canada • Germany • Hong Kong • Mexico • Singapore • United Kingdom

for (say) account enquiries are queued separately from calls to the sales number.

As well as handling the inbound calls, ACDs are typically the main source of management information in most call centres, producing statistics such as the volume of calls handled by each agent and the average and maximum time to answer calls. As an alternative to a dedicated ACD, many modern office PBXs can also have ACD functionality. Most telephone network operators are also able to deliver Intelligent Network (IN) services that provide a virtual ACD, without the need for equipment on the user's premises.

● **Interactive voice response (IVR) units.** These are increasingly used to automate basic processes. These answer inbound calls and present the caller with a range of options that can be selected using the telephone keypad (or increasingly by spoken response). As well as speeding up the response to inbound calls, IVR represents the final frontier in terms of call centre cost reduction. Avoiding the salary cost of a live agent reduces charges by around 90%, typically to 10¢ to 50¢ per call.

Call centre agents are invariably equipped with a desktop computer terminal. In most call centres the terminals are linked to the legacy back office system. The nature of these systems varies from industry to industry, but typically include reservations, billing and sales order processing systems.

A second generation of call centre technology is emerging with additional features and functionality. While frequently talked about, much of this technology is little used. Even an apparently mature technology such as CTI is only used in less than 10% of call centres.

> Like most solutions that involve IT investment, knowledge management systems can only act as tools within a wider business strategy

● **Computer telephony integration (CTI) software.** This can link the ACD to the back office system. This allows the caller's details to be displayed on the agent's terminal when the caller enters their account number (or even on the basis of calling line identity — the electronic transfer of the telephone number that the call originates from). CTI is often used with voice/data transfer, where an agent that needs to transfer a call can also simultaneously transfer the relevant customer data, streamlining hand-overs between agents.

● **Automated diallers.** These can be used to set up outbound calls. When an agent is free the dialler will make a call from a pre-programmed list, passing the call to the agent only if the called party answers. Predictive dialling takes this technology a step further, with the dialler anticipating the likely time when an agent will be free, aiming to establish the call at that instant. If the agent is not free, the called party may be put on hold, or the call dropped. (Understandably, consumer protection legislation constrains the use of predictive dialling in many countries.)

● **Voice recognition technology.** This is improving rapidly. Many new generation IVRs can respond to spoken commands and numbers, and progress is being made towards complete speech recognition.

● **Web integration.** This is attracting enormous interest. The principle is that a customer surfing the web can enter their telephone number and click a 'call me' button on a web page. This event is logged in the call centre, and the call is established — perhaps using an automated dialler — as soon as an agent is free. CTI allows the agent to see the web page that the caller was reading when they hit the 'call me' button. More sophisticated systems will even allow the agent to view the entire history of the caller's review of the web site.

● **Customer relationship management (CRM) systems.** Massive growth is predicted in the use of these software applications which interface with, or even replace, legacy back office systems. At the simplest level they allow the agent to

When it comes to your call center, we can help you tie all the pieces together.

The broadest suite of call center products.
The best lineup of industry-leading partners.
The solution you've been looking for to tie all the pieces together.

Find out more today.
Visit us at http://www.genesyslab.com
Call us at 1-415-437-1100 (Corporate Headquarters) or +44 1189 747000 (Genesys Europe)

GENESYS

perform the fulfilment activity — placing an order, performing an account enquiry or whatever. In addition, they also store the history of the caller's contact with the organization. Designed for use in call centres, most CRMs provide a more efficient agent interface, capturing — and presenting — more customer information than most legacy systems. Some CRMs focus on a particular niche application (for example, the Remedy helpdesk software). Other packages such as Vantive are non-specific and can be customized to meet a range of applications in most markets.

From transaction to relationship

Although call centre usage is growing and technology developments are keeping pace, the way call centre technology is often applied is causing problems.

In the same way that call centres were established to cut costs, new technology tends to be introduced for the same reason. IVR is implemented to cut staff numbers, CTI is used to improve efficiency and predictive dialling is used to take up slack staff time and speed up outbound calling. Cost reduction generates greater profitability, so these are all genuine benefits.

However, most call centres do not exploit technology to increase revenue. The inappropriate use of call centre technology can undermine revenue by failing to differentiate the service that high-value customers receive.

Customer value is an important concept. Literally, it is the net present value of the profit that a customer will create over the lifetime of a relationship with them, less the cost of acquiring them. In the call centre, this equation changes, as they have usually already been acquired. The cost of acquisition has therefore already been sunk and need no longer been considered.

The four key challenges in increasing customer value — and hence profitability — are:

● to understand the current and potential value of each customer;
● to ensure that high-value customers are retained;
● to maximize the potential for increase in the value of customers; and,
● to shed customers that have a negative value and no potential for growth.

Used properly — and most are not — the call centre has a pivotal role in achieving these goals.

First, the call centre is a critical tool for capturing information that allows one to understand the value of each customer. Every time a customer calls an agent to place an order, make an enquiry or even complain about a service, there is the opportunity to capture another piece of the customer-value jigsaw puzzle. In most call centres this valuable information is either discarded when the call ends, or irretrievably lost in legacy mainframe systems or even paper-based processes.

Used properly, a CRM can store all this information. More importantly, the data can be subsequently mined to identify high-value customers, and even those with a high potential value.

Separating the high rollers from those of lesser value is only the start of the process. The challenge then is to differentiate the service to retain the former, and lose the latter.

Before the call centre revolution, customer service did tend to differentiate between different value customers, if only in an *ad hoc* fashion. Based on their personal knowledge of the customers they were dealing with, staff in a branch office would make their own judgement of the value of a customer, and would tend to differentiate service levels accordingly. The big spender would be called into the manager's office; the time-waster would be left at the back of the queue.

Call centres removed this distinction, placing all callers in — literally — the same queue for the same level of service. Technology can now redress the balance, offering callers a service that reflects their business value.

I HAVE THAT INFORMATION
RIGHT HERE

DO YOU?

Emerging Technology Solutions International delivers call centre expertise and comprehensive solutions throughout Europe and the world.

Solutions that enable award-winning call centres for innovators such as BUPA and Halifax to transform data into information and a phone call into a personalised customer relationship.

Don't Keep Customers On Hold.
Hold on to your customers with real-time information and service.

Call us at +44 (0) 113 261 6500 or visit www.etsi-usa.com.
Windsor House, 1 Sovereign Quay, Leeds LS1 4DQ.
Tel: 0113 261 6500, Fax: 0113 261 6501

Managing the value of a customer
Service differentiation
New technology can redress this balance by differentiating service levels throughout the call centre.

Differentiating high and low value customers		
Stage	**High value customer**	**Low value customer**
Caller dials number	Allocate an exclusive toll-free number, available 24 hours x 7 days	Allocate a premium rate number available during limited hours
Call arrives at call centre	On the first call offer a choice of routes — operator, voice recognition or keypad operated IVR. Use the same route for all subsequent calls	Wherever possible, complete the call using keypad operated IVR
Call held in queue	Move calls to the front of the queue	Leave calls at the back of the queue
Call passed to agent	Allocate call to a highly trained pool of agents incentivized to deliver high quality service	Allocate call to a pool of agents incentivized to deal with calls quickly
Post-call	Follow-up where appropriate to ensure customer satisfaction	

To differentiate service in this way it is important that the call centre technology can differentiate between incoming calls, quickly separating the high value and low-value customers. There are three ways of doing this.

● **Allocating a separate number to each group**. The IVR can then allocate an inbound call to the appropriate queue or service, based on the number that the caller dialled.

● **Using CLI (also known as DNIS)**. Most telephone networks now pass the calling party's number to the called party. CTI systems can check this against the CRM database, and where there is a match determine which queue to place the call in. The problem with this system is that only around 50% of calls come with a valid CLI attached. Calls that originate in mobile networks, office phone systems or payphones may have a misleading or missing CLI.

● **Entry of a unique identifier**. Many IVR and CTI systems allow the caller to enter a unique number — usually their account number or a PIN code. This can then be checked against the database in the CRM, and used to determine which queue to place the call in.

None of these systems are perfect in allocating numbers — specific customer groups can be too coarse a grouping, CLI is unreliable, and entering a unique code can delay calls further. However, used selectively and sometimes in combination, they are the key to differentiating customer service.

Increasing customer value
The final challenge is to use the call centre to increase customer value. The key to this is to exploit the opportunities that the call centre creates for cross-selling products. Every time a customer calls, there is an opportunity to offer to sell additional services. The CRM plays a pivotal role in this process, identifying the products that the caller is most inclined to buy, based on their historic profile.

The CRM can also log the result of previous cross-selling activity — if a high-value customer turns down a product, one should not keep offering it every time they call. Cross-selling need not, and should not, be aggressive. As one is selling to an existing customer, the probability of a sale is high and the cost of the sale low. As blue chip retailers and financial services organizations have realized, this gives the scope to make generous offers to soften the process.

Enter the Internet

But the story does not end with the efficient use of the call centre. The arrival of the Internet is creating new challenges and opportunities for every call centre operator. The cost of selling over the Internet is around a tenth of the cost of selling via a call centre — even using IVR — making the Internet a channel that cannot be ignored.

The low cost of establishing an Internet presence can create a threat to established business. New market entrants can spring up overnight, and on the web it is hard to differentiate between an established multinational and a one-man operation.

A web presence will eventually be a must, but what does this mean for the call centre?

First, the web offers an alternative to the call centre. This is good for customers, and good for costs. Smart organizations will assess the impact this will have on their channel strategy. It should be possible to re-assess future call centre capacity — and hence costs.

One will also need to consider how to use the Internet to further differentiate between different value customers. An obvious response would be to restrict low-value customers to the Internet. However, the customer may place a high perceived value on the convenience of shifting to the net, so it may be worthwhile to offer the high-value customers the first chance to use the new service.

How to integrate both Internet and call centre channels will need to be considered. A simple example would be to use a 'call me' button on the web site. It is possible to go further, with integrated back office systems and call centre staff taking responsibility for the fulfilment activities associated with all electronic channels, not just the call centre. In future, this could extend to mass-market interactive television.

Additionally, as with the call centre, it is important not to forget the value of the customer information collected from the Internet. This should be integrated with the data collected via the call centre using the same CRM.

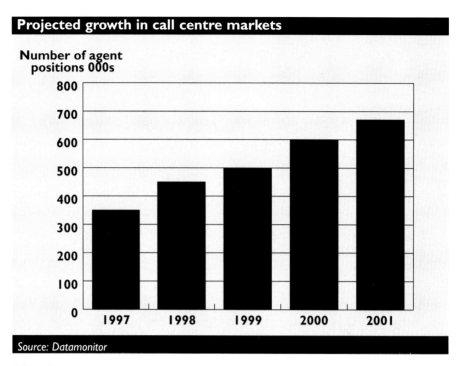

Projected growth in call centre markets

Number of agent
positions 000s

Source: Datamonitor

Key issues

As a general rule smart organizations:

● use their call centres to build up a picture of their customers;

● use the information they collect at the call centre to differentiate customer service, pampering the golden geese and slaughtering the turkeys; and

● are already planning to integrate the Internet into their call centre.

For those not at this level, the starting point for change should be a review of the existing call centre.

Key issues to consider are:

● Is customer information stored at a single point?

● Is customer data mined to segment customers, separating high and low value?

● Does the service differentiate between different value customers?

● Is technology being used to increase revenue, or just to cut cost?

● Is call centre performance measured in terms of customer value and revenue, or is it still measuring everything against the clock?

● How should the arrival of the Internet affect the call centre?

Although most organizations cannot answer all these questions, the review can be used to fill the gaps before prioritizing corrective action. Those short of ideas should try looking outside their industry to identify best practice.

Chapter 4: E-commerce

Overview

If one believes the hype, electronic commerce is about to take over the world. So are phrases like: "If you're not already into e-commerce, then it is probably too late", the new reality or just simple scaremongering?

One does not have to look too far for examples of e-commerce touching the lives of individuals as well as organizations. It sits behind retail transactions such as withdrawing cash from an ATM, or paying for goods at a supermarket checkout, which sets off an entire chain of stock replenishment transactions up the supply chain. It sits behind the vast majority of financial transactions, even if paper still fights a rearguard action. It underpins a whole range of non-transactions in not for profit organizations like government, health and defence.

Electronic commerce is the umbrella name given to a variety of ways of exchanging messages electronically. Its narrower, current definition excluding voice communication is "marketing and sales information communicated via digital messages between computers".

Electronic commerce has been around since the early 1960s, initially in the financial and travel industries. Organizations of all kinds transferred electronic data files internally and then with partners. The arrival of open message standards in the 1970s and 1980s saw a growth in EDI for business-to-business transactions, which never quite reached the expectations set for it.

High cost and poor ease of use are still cited as the barriers, and many organizations still make do with a bastardized form of EDI — printing out the message from one computer and re-keying it into another.

The recent hype about e-commerce coincides with the rise of the Internet. More specifically, the hype draws attention to the new channels of communication offered by Internet-enabled applications. The increase in PC usage by individuals and organizations means that one type of application — fast access to information world-wide by means of a web browser — has grown massively in barely half a decade.

There is no question that increasing the number and value of profitable customer relationships will drive superior financial performance

In a commercial environment that is relentlessly becoming customer-focused, organizations have little choice about deciding to use the e-commerce opportunities afforded by the Internet. It is a brave organization that decides nowadays that is has no need to use a web site as a means of communicating with its customers.

The importance of e-commerce is that it can:
- act as a substitute for traditional forms of information exchange, such as letters or telephone; and,
- re-engineer business processes, for example, just-in-time delivery in a fast response supply chain.

Both of these have an impact on the customer. Often it is the customer who is forcing the pace. Powerful customers forced their suppliers to use EDI in the 1980s. In the 1990s, the same customers expected their suppliers to communicate by e-mail, as well as by fax and phone calls.

Forward-looking businesses are now trying to see how they can protect and extend their customer base through e-commerce. This includes:
- establishing direct channels to customers, bypassing one or more links in the value chain;
- delivering new products and services in a way that was not feasible before;
- transcending geographical boundaries; and,
- redefining the way in which business is done in a community forum — electronically rather than by direct human interaction.

E-commerce applications and transactions

It helps to split e-commerce applications into two kinds: business and system/network.

The business applications support business processes directly. These are the screens, reports and background processes which process transaction data or which offer access to information in databases. The system/network applications provide the technical underpinning.

Business applications include:
- end-user applications, such as web browsers, e-mail and electronic forms; and
- under the surface applications, such as automated stock replenishment, and automatic data capture.

System/network applications and services include:
- directories;
- routing;
- network management;
- providing access to on-line information;
- EDI translation;
- network connection, protocol management;
- e-mail (X.400, Internet, WAN/LAN);
- archiving; and
- encryption and security.

The current interest in end-user applications reflects the interest in all things labelled Internet. Developments in other areas such as network management and security make fewer headlines but combine to allow e-commerce as a whole to move forward.

Instinctive Responses

Effective communication builds successful relationships

People communicate on countless levels. Who knows what will make us laugh, or cry, or reach out a helping hand? Such instinctive reactions seem a far cry from high technology. Yet call centres from Rockwell Electronic Commerce enable businesses to achieve unprecedented levels of Instinctive responsiveness to their customers.

At the same time, emergency services, charities and humanitarian agencies across the world have become more effective in their work thanks to the automatic call distribution technology pioneered by Rockwell.

Whatever the size of your organisation, Rockwell call centre solutions can transform the way you manage the relationships on which it depends. For more information, contact us using the communications medium with which you feel most comfortable.

For more information, please contact: Nigel Welsh, Rockwell Electronic Commerce Ltd, East Wing, Ground Floor, St Martins Place, Bath Road, Slough, Berkshire SL1 3UG
Tel: 0800 634 0200 Fax: 01753 876702 email: Info@ec.rockwell.com **www.ec.rockwell.com**

Four transaction types

An e-commerce business application makes use of up to four types of transaction or means of communication. They are:

● structured transactions between pre-arranged trading partners — for example: EDI;

● structured transactions between *ad hoc* trading partners — for example: e-forms;

● unstructured communication between *ad hoc* partners — for example: e-mail; and,

● access to and display of information — for example: a web browser.

The table below explains the characteristics of each type of transaction.

Characteristics of transformation types				
Structured data	Trading partners	Human involvement	Initiated by	Business application
Yes	Pre-agreed	No	Sender	EDI, client/server
Yes	Ad hoc	Yes and no	Sender	Catalogue orders, e-forms
No	Ad hoc	Yes	Sender	E-mail
No	Ad hoc	Yes	Recipient	Web browser

Every e-commerce application uses one or more of the above. Kiosk technology for example uses all four. Here the customer uses a smart card to sign on. This is a structured transaction between the client computer device in the kiosk and a central server. Next the customer is directed to a web page where a web browser shows today's special offers. Then the customer uses an e-form to place an order. Finally the supplier sends the customer an e-mail confirming when the order will arrive.

An understanding of these four types of transactions is important even though the customer is usually oblivious to them. This is because different technologies are used to handle each type of transaction, and each technology has its associated costs, risks and benefits. Business management must be in a position to understand what these are.

The following table maps some e-commerce business applications enabled by current and emerging technologies against the four transaction types.

Transformation types versus application technology				
Application technology	EDI Client/server	E-forms Agents	E-mail	Web browser
Home shopping	Yes	Yes	Maybe	Yes
Home banking	Yes	Maybe	Maybe	Yes
Interactive TV	Maybe	Yes	No	Yes
On-line auctions	Yes	Yes	Maybe	Yes

Issues from the new technology

Some of these technologies are more mature than others. Individuals have to decide how much time and effort they will invest in trying out a new technology. This raises a number of associated issues.

Management

Many of the issues surrounding e-commerce today are the same as those being discussed 10 years ago. That does not mean nothing has happened in the meantime. The debate has progressed, accompanied by both technical developments and the emergence of new requirements.

Application-to-application integration

Various questions need to be addressed. Does one expect the customer to do the work, for example typing in the order as if they were writing it out on an order pad? Or does one try to automate and remove the need for manual intervention?

(After all, a typical purchase replenishment application would expect to send out eight in 10 of its orders off to the supplier without any human input.) The rules are clear. Only exceptions need attention.

Some estimates of EDI usage (which is meant to be about one computer application exchanging messages directly with another, devoid of human interference) reckon that 70% of all supplier/customer EDI transactions require re-keying or human manipulation of some kind.

The use in recent years of web-based electronic forms to encourage smaller organizations and individuals to trade electronically merely continues the same basic problem: it takes considerable time and money to integrate e-commerce into an organization's computer systems.

Consultants and e-commerce devotees will maintain that it is worth the effort to change systems to match the business process more closely. They are generally right, but the majority of organizations have been inward looking up to now, failing to recognize external processes.

Customer focus changes this. It demands a different approach to justifying the development of integrated systems that support cross-functional and cross-organizational business processes.

Technology has also moved on over the last 10 years. The ability to develop application programming interfaces (APIs) has grown, helped by hardware-independent Java and Microsoft software. This allows different program objects to work together more easily. So the technology is less of an obstacle than before. The main question now is: does the management will exist to achieve application to application integration?

Reliability

Value added network (VAN) providers offer service level guarantees to their customers. They are in business to make sure there is sufficient bandwidth in their network to transfer messages in a predefined period of time. Reliability over the Internet has made great strides, but good statistics on Internet reliability are hard to come by.

Very few ISPs are willing to provide a cast iron 99.99% guarantee on delivery times — as yet. It will happen, as the distinction between the traditional, public Internet becomes blurred with intranets and virtual private networks set up for specific communities of users, guaranteeing an acceptable level of service.

Security

Individuals are wary of sending their credit card details over the Internet, yet they have complete trust in the public telephone system when making a credit card transaction. As with reliability, the issue of authenticity is being addressed. Certificates can now be attached to encrypted messages, providing a level of security which is more than adequate for most commercial purposes.

Legislation

The legal validity of an EDI invoice is something that ought by now to be clear cut. Yet it has taken years for the Belgian government to acknowledge the reality that a paper version of that invoice need never exist.

E-commerce takes individuals and organizations into uncharted waters legally. The implications of the US open stance on taxation of Internet transactions are still being debated in other parts of the world.

Ownership of data, copyright and trademarks is another area where legislation will fight to keep up. So, for example, what sanctions can be imposed on e-commerce operations which are based in unregulated safe havens?

The right to personal privacy is interpreted in different ways in different countries. The US and Europe have opposing views. Codes of conduct and

WIZnet: eCommerce™: the Internet business to business

WIZnet is one of the new generation of Internet products that show the usefulness of the World Wide Web as a valuable marketing tool.

Lately, anything that has to do with the Internet and Internet commerce seems to be headline news. Most of the excitement is directed toward consumer oriented applications that are changing the way people conduct their personal business. Now there is a strictly business application that is making news: it is the WIZnet eCommerce Portal™.

WIZnet eCommerce Portal™ is a serious Internet business-to-business solution for both buyers and sellers of products and services. WIZnet eCommerce Portal™ enables business buyers worldwide to select the exact item or service needed quickly and efficiently from more that 86,000 complete catalogs. It enables sellers to have their catalogs available to the business buyer anywhere in the world without requiring different paper and electronic versions. WIZnet eCommerce Portal™ further enables buyers to contact sellers and initiate transactions while they are still viewing the catalog page.

Rather than search through an industrial register or catalogs or make a series of phone calls to suppliers, business buyers can now rely on the resources of WIZnet eCommerce Portal™. The current business practice in sourcing and supply chain management is time consuming and paper intensive. It often does not result in the best quality, deliver or price terms.

The ideal solution would be a source that had the complete contents of every available catalog as it appears in the paper version, but on-line and completely searchable. That solution is WIZnet eCommerce Portal™. Using enabling technology exclusive to WIZnet, the search for a specific item or service can be quickly narrowed to the best possible sources. Once found, instant communications with the selected vendors is available through the completely integrated, secure email tool.

The internet development cycle is migrating from individual web sites to communities of web sites to fill different needs. This merger of web sites results in large web sites that contain massive amounts of data. WIZnet eCommerce Portal™ centralizes the data in one web site. It is all the web sites in one place.

It is not only a change in the ecosystem of the Internet it goes further than that. It is a paradigm shift from the paper society to the eCorporation. "What we are doing goes beyond simple technology enhancement," says Stephen Attansio, CEO and president at WIZnet. "It's a paradigm shift in the way that business to business works and will work. We offer all the benefits of the previous way of buying in terms of fit, form and functionality but have provided an extra dimension of benefits using web technology."

WIZnet eCommerce Portal™

WIZnet eCommerce Portal™ has as its foundation, the PurchasingExtranet and its interactive Virtual Catalog Library, a database of millions of catalog pages that is intuitively searchable using natural language queries. Catalogs are entered into the database either by scanning in the paper catalogs or by inserting the electronic file. No matter the source, all data is converted to Wiznet's advanced Electronic Commerce File (ECF) format which produces clear, crisp images. These images are then integrated into the interactive Virtual Catalog Library.

During the integration process the unstructured data on the pages are used to develop the self-organizing indexing structure. This process uses some of the most advanced adaptive pattern recognition process in use today. The indexing process is fully automatic and requires virtually no manual intervention. This allows the natural language query to return the exact form, fit and function as you would have using paper catalogs.

While this represents a massive library of product information, the query process is simplicity itself. The user types in natural language sentences to describe the product, features of the product or a supplier

THE
PURCHASING EXTRANET

name, e.g. "I want a $1/4$ inch brass ball valve." Specifying the geographical area or even the particular trade agreement can further narrow the search.

The search process will return a "hit list" of every supplier that has that product in their catalog as well as a line from that catalog that matches the query. When the user clicks on one of the lines in the "hit list" an exact image of that catalog page is displayed. Pages can be viewed forward and backward much as they would be if you had the catalog in your hand.

By clicking on the WWW button the user will be taken to the company's web site so they can gather background information. No need to copy and paste web site addresses, WIZnet eCommerce Portal™ automatically connects the user to the correct location. Alternately, the user can send secure e-mail containing attachments such as an RFQ, RFI or a purchase order directly from the selected catalog page. Again, no need to search for the correct e-mail address, WIZnet eCommerce Portal™ automatically inserts it.

For The Buyer

Whether the buyer is a purchasing professional, a supply chain manager, a design engineer, an importer, or a manufacturing or plant engineer, WIZnet's eCommerce Portal is the service of choice. The exact page of the suppliers catalog is instantly available, complete with specifications and data sheets. This reduces the amount of time the user must spend finding sources of products or services.

The time saved reduces the cost of each transaction. The reduced sourcing and purchasing lead-time results in decreased inventory, thus boosting overall productivity. Since all of the data from all suppliers is available in one place at one time it allows the user to make side-by-side comparisons. This can be a powerful negotiating tool. WIZnet eCommerce Portal™ is intuitive, it is instantaneous, it is global and it can be used on any Windows computer that has access to the Internet. It elevates the user to a new level of speed and performance. It is all business: no sports, no weather, no games, and no stock reports. It works with your current equipment, it requires no training of users, and no hand-holding. It is a serious business solution for the business buyer.

For The Seller

Original equipment manufacturers, distributors, exporters, contract manufacturers and service organizations for manufacturers can all make good use of WIZnet eCommerce Portal™. It is a powerful, immediate interactive and innovative sales and marketing channel. Because of WIZnet's global presence, its sales force and its marketing programs, the seller will be permanently exposed to a large number of qualified buyers anytime, anywhere. There are no geographic restrictions, no boundaries, no barriers of any kind.

Statistics:

86,000+ suppliers representing 100,000+ catalogs containing 475 million pages. 6000+ buyers from such companies as Boeing, Lockheed-Martin, Honeywell, General Dynamics, and the U.S. Air Force make 1,100,000+ product queries per month and send 41,000+ e-mails per month.

Since the sellers complete catalogs are entered into the database, they can reach a broader audience very cost effectively. There is no need to convert the catalog into some Internet compatible format that destroys the form and function of the original catalog. WIZnet helps suppliers effectively reach audiences that they could not reach previously due to geographic and resource limitations. Any business anywhere in the world that has Internet access can utilize the resources of WIZnet eCommerce Portal™.

The WIZnet audience is global and WIZnet eCommerce Portal™ is on the desktops of the people who use it. The engineers and purchasing professionals who use WIZnet's eCommerce Portal pay a fee to use the service, so they are serious about it. They use it to make decisions when they want to purchase a product or service and their choice is made from the online catalogs of WIZnet eCommerce Portal™.

History

Safwat Fahmy developed the idea of the eCommerce Portal in 1993 and founded WIZnet in 1995. Located in Delray Beach, Florida, WIZnet serves both buyers and suppliers globally, with clients in the Americas, Europe, Middle East and Asia.

Mr. Fahmy has more than 25 years experience in successfully developing and implementing a variety of innovative technology solutions. As a system architect, his computer science career spans a variety of essential positions at corporations including Goodyear, Combustion Engineering, and Baxter Travenoll. He has also served as an information consultant to IBM for many years.

Stephen Attansio, president and CEO, is a visionary in the electronic commerce field who joined WIZnet in 1998.

For subscription information, visit WIZnet at:

http://www.e-cportal.com
Worldwide Internet Solutions Network, Inc.
360 North Congress Avenue
Delray Beach, FL 33445, US
sales@wiznet.net 1-800-297-5377
Outside the US:
+1 (561) 272-7710
Fax: +1 (561) 272-2939

self-certification are considered appropriate in the US, with independent bodies auditing businesses' compliance with their self-imposed standards. The customer is expected to find out which businesses are safe. Europe is keener to adopt common legislation to punish organizations that break data privacy rules.

Work is underway to address all these e-commerce issues though it would be unreasonable to expect major breakthroughs on any one issue. The world is a long way from achieving global agreement overnight. Instead there will be a steady of trickle of improvements that smooth the path for e-commerce.

Drivers of adoption

The speed of take-up for a new product or service varies. Popular acceptance can be slow, fickle and eventually dismissive—until a number of criteria are met which lead to the product's success.

Marketing theory teaches that in all organizational groups there are people who are:

- early adopters, willing to try out a new product;
- late adopters, following the lead set by others and opening out into the mass market; and,
- never adopters, grudgingly using the by-now old product only when there is no other option.

Notable failures such as early versions of interactive TV, partial successes like EDI, and massive successes like the original Amstrad word processor illustrate the fact that a new technology product has to satisfy four criteria for it to appeal to the mass market. It must have the right technology infrastructure in place, be easy to use, correctly costed, and have the ability to meet a need.

> Use of e-commerce will remain a minority interest until the technology infrastructure becomes more widely used

Technology infrastructure

Participating in e-commerce is about more than having a PC. A business or an individual needs a reasonably modern and powerful PC, with up-to-date software and a tolerably fast network connection to begin to take part in any kind of e-commerce.

While most countries worldwide have achieved this for their major businesses, PC penetration among smaller businesses and consumers remains tiny in all but a few developed countries. The US has already reached household PC penetration of 40% (less than half with modems) while the major European countries have yet to reach 20%.

Consequently the use of e-commerce will remain a minority interest until the technology infrastructure becomes more widely used. The astounding rates of growth being experienced at present have their foundation in a very small starting point.

Other computing devices besides PCs may begin to take off. The arrival of digital television could be the lever to open up the market for TV set-top boxes — if someone can think up a suitable end-user application.

The highly successful French Minitel e-commerce system can perhaps be seen as an exception to this technology criterion. Its character terminals and slow transmission speeds look dated. Yet its high level of usage results from it hitting the next three criteria precisely.

Ease of use

Abundant curiosity and patience are needed to get over the learning curve of acquiring new ways of communicating and trading. This is especially true for the intrepid Internet shopper.

Using the example of consumer home shopping, today's on-line shopper could expect to use a virtual reality interface to select goods from a shelf in a store. Roaming through the virtual aisle, the shopper zaps the item on the virtual shelf and transfers it to the virtual shopping basket.

In contrast, the current implementations of on-line shopping are rather disappointing. The shopper scrolls through a long list of items with the dubious option of waiting a few seconds longer to see a two dimensional picture of the item.

When the on-line shopping experience takes longer than a trip to the store, then it is clear the application will not make the transition into the mass market. Some retailers will consider it worthwhile to add value to a small percentage of their key customers through an e-commerce application. For others, it will be a temporary distraction. They will bide their time until the technology, the business application and their customers' expectations for ease of use combine to make an e-commerce application a hit.

The ubiquity of the Internet means that it is the most likely vehicle for business-to business and business-to-individual e-commerce over at least the next five years

Even in the computer-literate business of selling business computer systems, ease of use has some way to go.

In a recent survey of computer equipment resellers, the UK computer magazine *PC Dealer* posed as a customer trying to order a humble inkjet printer via the resellers' web sites. They hit a number of problems — jargon like PO# and SKU, incomprehensible product codes, lack of information on availability and prices, and network and site congestion. The fastest purchase took around 15 minutes, the slowest half an hour. A comparable purchase made over the phone would take only five minutes.

Cost

The new product has to be affordable. It has to represent value for money. At the consumer end of the e-commerce market, this could mean getting hooked up to e-commerce as a useful by-product of buying an Internet-ready PC for under $750. The cost goes easily on a credit card. In a business context, the investment has to pay for itself either tangibly (reducing the costs of doing business) or intangibly (protecting revenue, fostering a better customer relationship).

Meeting a need

The jury is still out on how far an e-commerce application for consumer home shopping meets a real need. The concept is proven in some areas such as book, software and record purchases, but other areas are struggling.

The Amstrad word processor met a real need, since it allowed users to correct a typed letter before printing it. The desire to produce a clean, error-free document meant a lot to many quality-minded people.

Convenience is widely quoted as the overriding customer need. People are said to place a high premium on something that works faster, saving precious minutes of time.

While rapid response is a hallmark of modern e-commerce systems, assuming that a faster or more convenient product will acquire a mass following demonstrates a simplistic view of the complex needs of the customer. The distinction between shopping for necessities and browsing for luxuries shows up the fallacy of the time-saving justification alone.

Again, customer focus means recognizing that different customers have different needs. It implies taking a multi-channel approach to the market, with products and services tailored to meeting a number of minority needs. It implies taking the risk that many of these channels will remain oriented towards a minority of customers, and hoping that a few may grow into mass market channels — as the perceived need spreads.

Home banking is a good example here. Retail banks have encouraged their customers away from visiting local branches in several ways. Telephone banking (voice, voice response and touch-tone), enhanced ATM services and PC banking (direct, via Internet, integrated with financial management software like Quicken) have all been tried, sometimes more than once.

The first generation of touch-tone banking failed to reach a critical mass. It was too fussy and unfriendly to use. The features available in the second generation (such as transfers between accounts, and bill payment) mean that it is now quicker and more convenient for the user than placing a voice call to a customer service agent. The need for fast, accurate, customer-controlled transactions is being met in an improved way.

E-commerce into the future

Some e-commerce avenues will blossom. Others will be dead ends. Two avenues look like clear favourites for the next five years:

● on-line Internet, which supports three out of four of the e-commerce transactions mentioned; and,

● traditional EDI, which encompasses the steadily increasing requirement for the formal, clear-cut transfer of information between two organizations.

Internet

The ubiquity of the Internet means that it is the most likely vehicle for business-to business and business-to-individual e-commerce over at least the next five years. E-mail is the key driver for individuals and organizations to obtain Internet access.

From here it is a question of how far these individuals and organizations can be tempted away from existing paper-based, or human-interaction methods of doing business, and into a method based on screens, user interfaces, keyboards and task-specific Internet access devices.

As users go on-line, they seek comfort in familiarity. This means using famil-

iar search engines to find what they want, and it means using familiar entry points or portals. The comparison to an all-under-one-roof department store or shopping mall is striking.

Familiarity is closely related to brand strength, and organizations are beginning to develop web-based loyalty programmes to encourage their growing number of on-line customers to return. Recognizing loyal customers from their e-mail addresses and passwords is the easy part. The difficult part is configuring marketing offers that compete effectively for the attention of an increasingly knowledgeable and demanding customer.

Internally, organizations will use web technology to support their processes, at the same time blurring previously well defined functional and organizational boundaries.

Sharing data is one thing, processing it through an application that allows it to be used as information is another.

The Internet has opened up access to information in a way that was unimaginable only 10 years ago. Progress has been much slower in the area of intelligent agents that perform tasks under the surface and without human interaction. This is currently the province of application-to-application EDI.

Traditional EDI

Predictions of the death of EDI have been widespread since the Internet began to grow. Paradoxically, the raised expectations among trading partners for fast, efficient and reliable exchange of information can only be met through EDI. The widely accepted ANSI and EDIFACT standards for message formats may be cumbersome, but there is no other *lingua franca* that comes close.

Little progress beyond talk of using XTML (extended text markup language) to define message contents in a more Internet-standard way, means that implementation is several years away.

Closer relationships between customers and suppliers that depend on the exchange of structured information will confirm the use of EDI for application-to-application communication. The problems of interfacing and integrating data have been with us since the start of the computer age. They are not about to disappear.

know. act.

Knowing what is driving business gives you the power to influence where it goes. Cognos puts that power in the hands of every manager within your organisation. Our world-leading Business Intelligence software lets managers access and analyse multidimensional corporate data whenever they need it. To reveal hidden relationships. To spot key trends and opportunities. To plan more effective strategies. To make better decisions, every day. Find out how Cognos Business Intelligence can impact your bottom line within 90 days by asking for a free copy of The Multidimensional Manager, your FREE authoritative guide to implementing Business Intelligence in your organisation. Call 07000 4 264667 or visit our web site.

The MULTI DIMENSIONAL MANAGER
24 WAYS TO IMPACT *your* BOTTOM LINE *in* 90 DAYS

www.cognos.com

COGNOS®
Better Decisions Every Day ™

Chapter 5: Customer information management

Overview

Companies are increasingly seeking to build lifelong relationships with their customers and that relationship can only be facilitated by learning what that customer values highly. The answers to fundamental questions — such as "what trust and value do customers have in your company?" and its corollary, "how much are they prepared to pay for it?" — now dictate how companies have to differentiate products and services from their competitors.

Much of this increased information about customers would not be possible without the recent changes in consumer and corporate culture and developments in sophisticated IT solutions such as smart cards, call centres and e-commerce. Consumers are becoming ever-more sophisticated in their demands and companies are being forced to respond with even better service offerings. However, the technologies that make large volumes of customer data available must be complemented with sophisticated tools, that turn this information into knowledge that can be applied.

The marketplace

In the last couple of years there has been an explosion in information derived from retail store, banking and travel service loyalty schemes. While the arguments rage over whether these schemes have increased customer loyalty, the amount of valuable customer information gathered at each transaction cannot be disputed.

Increasingly this information will be used to segment customers into groups with common needs, allowing more tailored communication, product development, advertising, pricing and promotions. Apart from generating products aimed at suiting each customer's lifestyle better, companies are using their increased knowledge of their customers to provide:

- a more personalized service (preferences are recorded, questions are not repeated);
- preferential treatment to profitable customers;
- loyalty rewards; and,
- access to additional services (such as club lounges or community web sites).

Involvement by industry sector

The table below highlights the impact which greater levels of customer information will have on the landscape of various industries.

Effects of customer information by industry		
Industry sector	**Knowledge**	**Source**
FMCG companies/manaufacturers	• What to make • Which retailers to deal with • Brand strengths/weaknesses	• Retailers • Customer complaints service • Research/audit organisations • Web sites • Product development
Banking	• Which customers to offer services to • Which services to offer • Better investment decisions	• Customers' service usage • Customers' requests • Strategic realationship with retailers/telecoms comapnies
Retailing	• Whose products to stock • Where to site stores • What strategic relationships to form	• Loyalty card information • EPOS transactions • Manufacturer liaison • Web sites • Research/audit organizations
Utilities/telecoms	• Service usage patterns • Billing preferences • Public perception • Customer level of product/ service knowledge	• Service usage • Research/audit organizations • Loyalty schemes • Churn level figures
Public sector	• Public opinion/issues • Level of knowledge of general public • How to offer cost effective public information	• Survey returns • Web sites • Customer service information
Media organizations	• Public opinion • Products to commission • Level of media consumer knowledge	• Viewing/circulation figures • Surveys • Customer complaints

The trend of new technologies to help focus on customer needs has been complemented by a number of business trends.

Top management has spent much of the last five years focused on internal restructuring and cost cutting, in preparation for new international markets and competitors. Although this work necessarily continues, it is no longer at the top of everyone's agenda. Companies are beginning again to make their relationships with customers central to their business plan. Interest in the potential of technological tools is also heightened by the results of numerous mergers, joint ventures and strategic alliances.

In the past year there have been record levels of company mergers. As well as the financial and logistical issues raised, massive information resources from each party need to be brought together. In the short term this will be a complex and difficult task, but should lead, in the long term, to a better understanding of the customer.

Increasingly strategic alliances may allow small companies to access a much larger organization's customer base or large organizations to target a specific group of potential customers which have previously eluded it. Customer intelligence plays several key roles in this partnering process:

● giving information on who to partner with;
● providing modelling of the likely impact of the partnership; and,
● generating a fusion of customer information between partners to create a more complete whole.

Other business trends contributing to the uptake of knowledge management disciplines and decision support tools include:

● **Cost savings**. The underlying cost of conducting business will always be key to success. Knowing the customer and how best to reach them can lead to cost savings. Savings can be made, for example, by maximizing the effectiveness of advertising, saleforce activities and pricing.

● **Customer segmentation**. Increasingly effective segmentation models, possibly driven by the micro-segmentation possible in e-commerce transactions, will allow organizations to target products or services at particular customer groups.

● **The adoption of technology**. Tools such as smart cards and e-commerce are being used more and more as customers become familiar with the technology and the benefits it delivers.

> Like most solutions that involve IT investment, knowledge management systems can only act as tools within a wider business strategy

The technologies involved

The problem for senior management is how to assess customer intelligence and knowledge management without an in-depth understanding of the technologies involved.

Like most solutions that involve IT investment, knowledge management systems can only act as tools within a wider business strategy.

Deciding where more information would be useful — or how the development of new products can be improved — is the first step in this process. Only then can technical solutions be matched to these needs. The technologies will then fall into two categories — technologies used in the collection of customer information and those designed for its subsequent analysis and communication.

Many of the technologies that will furnish data are covered elsewhere in the book (see chapters on e-commerce and call centres). However, others include:

● **Smart card technology**. This offers credit card sized devices with an amount of storage and computing power. These are being utilized for applications such as loyalty cards, credit cards, identification cards or even as electronic purses carrying money electronically. They allow secure, unique identification of individuals and organizations while providing the owner with additional functionality.

● **Electronic point of sale (EPOS)**. This equipment has become increasingly sophisticated over the last five to 10 years. Most major retailers' tills are now networked and give a real-time insight into sales and store activity. This can now be combined with a collection of loyalty card information, payment clearance and the production of discount vouchers.

How PowerCenter made sparks fly for Birmingham Cable

Informatica's PowerCenter product shows that data manipulation and its warehousing can be readily integrated into existing systems as this case study shows.

Birmingham Cable, holder of the UK's largest single cable franchise, is one of the country's leading providers of telecommunications. To date, the company has invested almost £350 million to build a state-of-the-art network that is delivering advanced telecommunication, information and entertainment services in Birmingham and Solihull.

The main network is now complete and more than 470,000 homes and businesses in the franchise area have access to Birmingham Cable's communication services. More than 160,000 residential customers and 4000 businesses are enjoying the benefits of these services.

Last year, the company's management ordered the migration of customer data from a subscriber management system (SMS) supplied by one vendor to another. The data transformation process needed to be automated, consistent and swift. Birmingham Cable chose Informatica's PowerCenter to facilitate and manage the conversion. In addition, Birmingham Cable plans to use PowerCenter as its platform to deploy data warehouses and data marts across the enterprise.

Three years ago Birmingham Cable employed external consultants to build a bespoke warehouse that was front-ended by a Visual Basic application and back-ended by SQL and PL*SQL scripts.

Vinay Balsara, strategic systems manager for Birmingham Cable, provides the background. "That project was not a success for Birmingham Cable as the warehouse became more and more out of line with the operational SMS. It proved difficult to reconcile the two systems. The main problem was that the 'exceptions' were not realised in the program logic of the operational system when the external consultants interviewed internal staff to draw up specifications."

Further ineffectual attempts were made to create a sales and marketing warehouse but it was only in the summer of 1997 Balsara became aware of PowerMart while attending a Business Objects User Conference. Impressed by the product's functionality, he developed a proof-of-concept campaign to sell it internally at Birmingham Cable.

"We used PowerCenter to mimic a warehouse that was already in place and to see how quickly we could replicate the functionality of SQL scripts within the product. We also used Accurate, another partner of Informatica, to assist with the development. The proof-of-concept project lasted 10 days. Within this timeframe, we were able to replicate the functionality of the SQL scripts, which took six weeks to develop. The product proved a success. It was fast, reliable and did what we wanted it to do."

But the proof-of-concept project did not justify PowerCenter's purchase alone. "We were told we had to do a migration from our current subscriber management system to a new application. Having to migrate data from Oracle/AIX to DB2 on OS/400, we decided that we could use PowerCenter to read Oracle tables and write to flat files. We started using it then and we are successfully doing so now."

Birmingham Cable's initial capital investment in Informatica's PowerCenter was substantial. However, the product's functionality led to clear-cut business value.

Balsara says, "PowerCenter's benefits allowed us to rapidly move data around, and the skills required to use PowerCenter were relatively basic. You didn't need the nitty, gritty PL/SQL skills. The product is more intuitive and graphical. We were in short supply of people who were proficient with PL/SQL programming and were knowledgeable of the database layout.

"We needed to find a solution that could compensate for this deficiency in skills. In addition, the speed of development using PowerCenter was 10 times faster than trying to generate something in a 3GL equivalent, which proved a great benefit. The bottom line is that the product had paid for itself within a few months."

Birmingham Cable may source and target Oracle Financial applications, and a Decision Support System in the future. Ultimately Birmingham Cable will conduct a full conversion during a two to three day period. For development purposes, the company currently runs its mappings or sessions on an ad hoc basis.

"We have a series of mappings," says Balsara. "We run them when we need to. It is an iterative process, and we have a test database that contains a subset of 5000 customers, allowing us to develop in a controlled environment."

"When we run against our live database, we will be running against 50,000 houses, and 150,000 customers within these properties. Each customer can take a particular service, cable television and/or cable telephone. We are running against sources that can generate millions of rows.

"For example, one of the mappings converts all telephone calls from customers for a given month. Each month represents 20 million rows. That particular mapping had to deal with volume, but relatively low levels of complexity. Other mappings are far more complex. The different levels of complexity and volume within the 50 or so mappings resulted in processing throughput ranging from over 1000 records per second to less than 10."

"From the staging areas we will use PowerCenter to create the target tables for the warehouse. Business Objects and also neural network technology will then access the warehouse." ∎

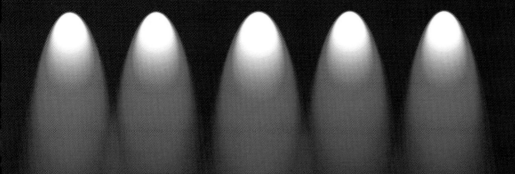

..and the winner is......

- **ATMs**. These are also becoming more sophisticated in the same way as EPOS terminals. Many companies believe that these terminals will form part of a future vision of electronic commerce.
- **Workflow and groupware applications**. These are increasingly being used within organizations as an effective means of automating the flow of business processes. What these packages also allow organizations to do is capture and store information during business processes, for later retrieval or incorporation into more sophisticated business models.

The technologies which take all this data and translate it into useable knowledge fall into four main categories — data warehouses, reporting tools, data mining tools and pattern matching tools.

Data warehouses

These are basically giant databases holding large amounts of information. This information is gathered from various sources, including:
- transactional/finance systems (eg Oracle Financials, SAP);
- historic performance data (eg profit/loss balance sheets);
- marketing databases/research (eg Nielsen, IRI);
- customer service systems (eg complaints tracking, call centres); and,
- external information providers (eg demographic information, market predictions).

Reporting tools

Reporting tools are used to produce basic or standard reports from information in the data warehouse. This often proves more convenient than producing such reports from the system from which the information came.

Data mining tools

These are more sophisticated reporting and analysis applications. They are used to "drill" (hence the name) into the huge repository of data held in the data warehouse and extract nuggets of information. Typically most value will be added by analyzing the relationships between information which came from different sources and which could not previously be carried out.

Pattern matching tools

These are a relatively new addition to the set of tools used to develop knowledge. These applications often use artificial intelligence techniques such as fuzzy logic, expert systems or neural networks which until several years ago were very basic or confined to academic computer departments because of the sheer computing power needed to run them.

These applications are often used with data mining tools. Whereas data mining tools drill down to extract existing information, pattern matching tools attempt to draw recognizable patterns out of large volumes of data. These patterns can then be used either in a comparative way (say, 1996 sales versus 1997 sales) or in a predictive way (for example, 1991 sales + 1991 economic model provides predictions for 1999 sales + economic model).

The opportunities and threats

It is easy to spend a great deal of money on customer information management and decision-support solutions. Making that investment pay, however, is not simple and, to do so, clear objectives are needed otherwise large amounts of money can be wasted on expensive information gathering systems which do not deliver any insight.

By using the right customer information management techniques based on sound knowledge management techniques, it is possible to become a market

leader by delivering what the customer wants. It is also possible to learn more about competitors' strategies and their likelihood of success, and make more informed decisions about new product and service development.

Time is of the essence as more advanced competitors are likely to steal market share and customers and the threat of technological advance in this area is ever increasing. Organizations now occupying different parts of the supply chain are gaining more experience of knowledge management technologies. They know that opportunities will arise for them to leap-frog much of the value chain and start developing direct relationships with new customers.

This means that:

● for goods manufacturers there is a risk of being at the mercy of retailers who strengthen their position in the eyes of the consumer;

● for retail banks, more targeted offerings by competitors may represent lost income; and,

● for utilities, any means that a competitor finds for reducing billing costs or increasing customer service may represent a threat.

Commercial and practical uses

A number of practical issues must also be addressed once the decision to pursue more customer knowledge has been made. For organizations, these issues will include:

● **What is the best way to gain valuable customer data?** This could be by capturing more information during business processes, gathering additional customer data oneself or buying in information from a strategic partner;

● **Who owns the customer in the organization?** It could be marketing, sales, billing departments or another group;

● **Who owns the ultimate consumer of the goods and services?** This may be a different individual or organization than the direct customer, for instance some fast-moving consumer goods (FMCG) companies see retailers as the "customer" and shoppers as the "consumer";

● **Is the organization making full use customer data when it has it?** Significant amounts of information may already exist, but not be properly collated, analyzed or stored. Doing this may offer an initial way forward without major investment in information providers or loyalty schemes; and,

● **What is the competition doing?** Do they have loyalty cards, data warehousing and micro-segmentation of their customers?

The five pillars of customer information management

Ownership and management

The key to any successful customer information management initiative is the efficient management of data, information and learning/knowledge. Closely linked to this is identifying information owners who take responsibility for the information and are in a position to answer queries from elsewhere in the organization.

Data into knowledge

Transforming data into knowledge gives data its value to an organization. Data is a basic record. Information is a group of connected items of data. Knowledge is information from which insight has been drawn.

Any organization can buy data, it is what its staff do to the obtained data to transform it into knowledge that will set it apart from the information its competitors have.

The virtuous circle

All business processes benefit from adopting a virtuous circle model. This term describes the capture of learning, the storage or learning and, most importantly, the re-application of this learning in later cycles of the process. This should lead to a constant, albeit gradual, evolution of knowledge and business process.

The learning organization

The learning organization is one where learning captured either through transforming data, the virtuous circle or some other means is freely communicated between the function that owns the knowledge and other functions. This depends on the corporate culture and a sufficiently robust technical infrastructure to support this process. A key success factor in this is overcoming the information-is-power mindset.

Organization and people

Customer information management is not just an IT discipline. To succeed, any customer information management initiative needs to convince both the organization and its people that this kind of information and knowledge sharing is the right way forward.

The next step

The key stages required to realize the benefits of customer information management are detailed below. These can be used as a template for further investigation and implementation.

Customer information management strategy

No one knows how a company works better than its own staff. The development of a customer information management strategy will create a vision of how to maximize existing information resources, develop new systems (IT or otherwise) and alter company culture to facilitate greater customer intelligence.

Customer intelligence assessment

Many organizations already have vast sources of information which are either under-utilized or not recognized at all. These sources could range from legacy databases of product shipments to 35 years of on-the-job experience as a member of a sales team. Other areas of information may be lacking, either because they have not been felt to be sufficiently relevant or have proved difficult to obtain in the past.

An in-depth analysis of where an organization's customer intelligence strengths and weaknesses lie will enable a more holistic model of information needs and resources to be developed.

Implementation

An IT system will almost certainly be required to collate, harness and communicate information and knowledge. Setting data and communication standards along with planning application integration will be key to this process. A good first stage in the implementation planning process would be to examine the technologies highlighted in this chapter in more depth.

Cultural change

As with most projects, the people affected by the change in working practices or systems need to be won over. This can be difficult, particularly when trying to convince staff who have hoarded information to start sharing it — and even more so when staff feel that giving information away may endanger their position.

Communication of a customer information management strategy along with staff involvement in its development are key to overcoming these fears.

Realizing the benefits

Effective customer information management and improved customer intelligence do not come cheap, and generally do not lead to immediate cost savings. Where benefits can be realized is in product development, customer satisfaction and the level of staff morale.

But how can one measure these benefits to decide whether the strategy has been a success? Some potential measurable benefits are:
● Product development — reduced time to market or increased levels of product innovation;
● Customer targeting — reduced number of products or more products targeted at specific customer groups;
● Customer satisfaction — increase repeat purchases or market share;
● Operational savings — reduction in staff required to research, filter and distribute information, or a time saving for each member of staff who requires access to specific information; and,
● Staff morale — reduced turnover of staff.

Evolution

Once the customer information management strategy has been implemented and the staff are comfortable with both the strategic vision and the way that their work processes have been transformed, this is only the beginning! Once that learning and ideas flow more freely, more staff time can be devoted to targeting and innovation rather than searching for information.

A customer information management strategy will evolve over time as an organization changes; however the overall objective of better customer intelligence to facilitate knowing, developing, and serving customers and building long-term profitable relationships will remain.

In the interim, four key questions for any organization remain:
● Where does customer knowledge come from ?
● Is full usage of the information on customers being made?
● Are there ways of gathering more customer information either directly from the customer or via third parties?
● How can huge amounts of customer data be manipulated to generate profitable knowledge?

Chapter 6: Sales force automation

Overview

Selling is traditionally seen as a communication between the seller and the buyer with the buyer as the passive recipient of the sales patter. This is changing. It is the buyer who now makes the choice about whether to initiate and follow through a sales process. Information is not limited to contact with the salesforce, it may be only a few seconds away using a mouse-click or a telephone call.

This means that the role of the external salesforce is in the process of dramatic change. They are no longer the focal point of contact between a business and its customers. The sales person now represents just one of several such points — the customer service agent on the telephone, the business development manager at head office, the inanimate web site — and may not even be the most important point of contact.

The gradual automation of the sales process is set to continue. Trends include:

● the continuing shift from external to internal salesforces;

● the greater use of technology, especially when the front office customer service agent can tap into the knowledge contained in large customer databases;

● senior management learning how to achieve the optimum balance between control over the sales process and empowerment for the individual seller and buyer, so they can transact business in a successful non-standard way; and,

● removal of the intermediary in the sales process.

External and internal salesforces

One of the trends of the last 10 years has been the shift indoors of the salesperson. Business managers have quickly woken up to the fact that an internal, telephone-based salesperson can achieve similar results to an external salesperson — and at a fraction of the cost. Motivation of internal sales teams has now become as sophisticated as motivation of external sales teams.

Early experiments resulted in friction between the internal and external salesforces. Turf battles were fought. Business learned accordingly and compromised by setting up teams of external and internal salespeople targeting the same accounts. The customer benefited from greater sales contact, admittedly by telephone with fewer visits, and the business benefited from a more efficient use of resources.

The increased use of internal salesforces has been made possible by the willingness of customers to accept a telephone call as the equivalent to a sales visit. For some customers, it is even more convenient. They make the call when it suits them and they appreciate speaking to the same person. The customer relationship is friendly, even if the internal salesperson never gets to meet the customer.

Technology used by the salesforce

The salesforce's first encounter with technology used to come in the form of reports, usually voluminous sales reports describing product sales by customer, customer sales by product, customer group sales by TV region and the like. But even the IT departments recognized eventually that sales people could only carry so much paper around with them, and began to look more at the kind of information that a sales person could properly use.

Better telecommunications allowed replacement of mailed reports and computer disks by file transfer using modems. The data had to be kept small because of bandwidth limitations, something which still applies today. Portable computer technology has improved to the point that today's salesforce is likely to make use of the following business and technical functions.

Business functions include:

- campaign management;
- lead tracking;
- call planning;
- contact management;
- quote configuration and monitoring;
- diary management;
- activity statistics — visits, sales; and,
- team working.

Technical functions include:

- remote synchronization of data, data propagation;
- security;
- integration with other PC software; and,
- screens, data views and reports all configurable by the user.

Salesforce systems themselves now form part of a new generation of software known as customer relationship management (CRM) software. Such software recognizes that an organization has many contacts with a customer, and that a more holistic approach is required to deal with them. Hard and soft data about the customer is recorded in large customer databases, and analysis tools are used to present this data back in the form of usable information which can be used directly in the sales call. For example, the customer's recent buying patterns may indicate a change of direction that the customer service agent can exploit.

> Best practice salesforce business systems try to achieve a balance between empowerment and control

Accurate data

Data presents an enormous challenge in salesforce automation projects. All implementations require the loading of customer and product related data into tools such as opportunity management systems, electronic product catalogues, product and pricing configurators, quotation generators and so on. As well as the master file information, the transaction and contact information has to be up-to-date. Doing this involves answering questions like:

- What data do we need?
- Where does the data exist?
- Is the data accurate?
- How does one maintain the data? Whose changes take precedence?
- How can the authenticity of the data be confirmed?

Data is often held in more than one place. Information about a single customer can be at the head office and on the mobile computers of the regional manager, the area manager and the sales representative. When the customer phones in with a complaint to head office, the information has to be passed on. When the sales representative investigates and resolves the complaint, the details have to be communicated — from the salesperson's PC to the centre and then back out again to the other two PCs.

This sort of synchronization (also known as replication or propagation) is not easy. The volumes of data can be large. Conflicting updates have to be handled.

Changes in sales territories lead to reassignment of customers to sales representatives. Half of sales rep A's customers now move to sales rep B, and half of their customers move to sales rep C. The databases at the centre and on each PC have to be reorganized accordingly.

Good salesforce automation software can handle these issues. It helps if management — or more specifically, the database administrator — is fully aware of what the implications are of such changes, and knows how to ensure that they have been implemented correctly.

Finding the correct methodology

Some software packages follow a strict sales methodology. They support a single way of selling, a single sales process. The salesperson's instinct is to fight back against this inflexibility. To concentrate on a single process violates the fundamental customer-focused approach of sales. It is nearly impossible to determine what will be necessary on the next customer call, and therefore defining, for instance 17 steps in the process only causes more work for the salesperson to decipher what the tool is asking for — or how to beat the system.

Successful salesforce automation projects tend to make use of individual tools that will assist sales calls and that can be reused from call to call. Examples of tools that can be adapted are a configurator capability and perpetual client history management. Examples of tools that do not necessarily work are built-in sales methodologies and lock-step process decision trees.

Best practice salesforce business systems try to achieve a balance between empowerment and control. This means that there are certain items of customer information that the sales person can change, and there are other items which only, say, the finance department can amend. The sales person can see gross and net revenues for their customers, but only gross revenues for customers looked after by others.

The sales process is dynamic because it is customer-focused. It follows that the supporting business systems have to be flexible and supportive. What works for sales person 'A' may not necessarily be what sales person 'B' requires — not because of behavioural differences between sales person 'A' and 'B', but because customer expectations are different.

A good example of the dilemma this poses is the arcane area of telephone script development. The customer service agent must go through a standard set of script steps, to maintain consistency and provide a lowest common denominator level of service to the customer. However, the customer service agent is motivated to inject personality, creativity and innovation into the telephone conversation, and the computer system must allow this. Is deviating from the script acceptable? Sometimes, yes, because it is driven by the customer and may lead to closing a sale.

Motivation and management

Money remains a powerful motivator. Every sales person who is on a commission or incentive scheme should know exactly where they stand regarding how much they have earned so far this period. Their computer system should be able to tell them about:

- revenue, units;
- margin;
- commission;
- outstanding items, such as customers who have not paid their bills; and
- their standing relative to their colleagues.

This information should show up on the screen. It should be instantaneous, allowing the sales person to compare performance this period against target or against the last period. If the system does not do this, then the sales person will spend the time doing it anyway, to the detriment of the sales process.

Another powerful motivator is management. The telesales person knows that the supervisor may be listening into a call at any time. Their activity on the telephone and computer is logged and can be analyzed. The external salesperson has a little more freedom, but daily contact with head office for exchanging call reports and e-mails means that managers can exercise quite tight controls. Slippages in performance can be spotted quickly.

Common difficulties

Providing automation for the external salesforce has its dangers. There are the obvious ones, such as the loss of an expensive PC or if valuable data falls into the wrong hands, especially when a disgruntled salesperson is about to leave.

Focusing on the technology and paying insufficient attention to the processes (tasks, results, measurements) and the organization (training, change of culture, leadership) will create implementation problems in the same way as for any other project.

Other pitfalls are more subtle. One mobile PC solution was excellent in every respect but one. The software had been designed with the users, so it was flexible and convenient. It could set up visit schedules whenever required, and the customer sales and contact information was synchronized with the central computer daily. Call reports were uploaded and sales statistics reports were downloaded automatically. E-mails were exchanged. One salesperson found the system to be unusable. The reason? Each night at 3am in the morning, the mobile computer dialled out to the central computer to send and receive data. It was plugged into the telephone socket in the bedroom and it proved impossible to silence the dialling tones and whistles.

Automation out of existence?

Unkind souls will comment that true salesforce automation means doing away with the salesforce altogether: the salesforce becomes automated out of existence. Concepts such as self-serve buying put the power directly in the hands of the buyer and take the sales representative out of the loop — another casualty of disintermediation.

Financial transactions such as bank accounts and insurance policies can be arranged over the Internet, with wizards to help explain what needs to be completed. Help is at hand via e-mail or, as a last resort, by telephone.

This trend will continue. Sales channels that cost less than traditional human sales channels include:

- self-serve kiosks and machines;
- PCs over the Internet, interactive TV;
- touch-tone telephone; and
- direct mail, fax and e-mail.

The trick is to shift the time cost on to the customer. The customer will often accept this inconvenience in return for the choice it provides — when to buy, where to buy and how to buy.

The external and the internal salesperson will not die out altogether. There are several reasons for this.

- **Human interaction**. Some sections of society will continue to choose to do business in a low-tech manner. They may have to pay a premium for the face-to-face contact, but they will appreciate the personal, human service that they receive. Some transactions have to be done in person. Making an estimate for double glazing requires a sales visit, since house statistics are rarely held in reliable digital format.
- **Legislation**. A few products and services are still too complex to sell without a human explaining the pros and cons, and reacting to the buyer. The consumer needs protecting and the best way to do this is to make an individual accountable, not a computer program. Pension selling is an example of this.
- **Changing roles**. Selling will not be the only role that changes. Salespeople already take on other customer-focused roles such as customer research, customer service and business development. As well as selling or supporting existing products and services, they are finding out the next range of products that will be attractive to their customers. They are asking their customers questions. The answers are captured, analyzed, and may result in the computer suggesting a series of follow-up actions for the salesperson.

Chapter 7: Consumer goods, retailing and manufacturing

Overview

There are huge changes and challenges ahead as the retailing and manufacturing industry becomes more sophisticated and more data-rational in its decision-making.

Retailers will fight ever harder to win the hearts and minds of consumers and shoppers, both through existing retail channels and newly emerging technology-enabled channels. The use of technology to capture, manage, analyze and exploit information about consumers and shoppers will be fundamental to this.

At the same time, the new channels will potentially open up the market in the interests of the consumer, of diversity, and of smaller more specialist manufacturers.

Mainstream manufacturers face a considerable challenge. Objective category planning driven by deep consumer and shopper insight will no longer allow shelf-space for products that are insufficiently differentiated or lack critical mass in terms of consumer demand.

This will result in a rationalization of the range and the supplier base. Only those manufacturers with strong brands and market share in their core categories, strong own-label manufacturing businesses, or a profitable niche can view this with any equanimity. There will also be an increase in marketing support for key brands, and a strong emphasis on improving payback on marketing and trade promotion investment through better targeting of the consumer.

Both manufacturers and retailers will place product innovation high on the list of their strategic priorities and will leverage their increased understanding of the consumer and shopper to improve launch success rates and speed to market. One of their great challenges will be how to balance the economic necessity to develop once and roll-out globally with the need to be ever more responsive to local consumer and shopper needs.

The winners in the fast-moving consumer goods sector will be those organizations that understand their customers — whoever they are — and have the ability to respond rapidly to their evolving requirements at minimum cost. This requires entrepreneurial vision, and embracing a commitment to exceed customers' expectations.

It requires close customer relationships along the entire demand and supply chain from primary industry to supermarket shelf and to the consumer. This will in turn be facilitated by powerful information systems and broad information sharing.

The components
The consumer

The consumer is becoming ever more demanding. Guaranteed availability, outstanding quality and freshness, and value for money are all now taken for granted as the norm. These expectations are generally being met. Product variety and innovation are becoming more important, convenience foods are playing a more important role in people's busy lives and tastes are evolving to embrace a more diverse range of products from different ethnic backgrounds.

The trend towards a healthier lifestyle and healthier eating habits is also having a greater and greater influence over consumer buying habits. Retailers understand these trends and are responding by offering products carefully tailored to meet changing consumer demands.

Environmental friendliness and social responsibility by the producer are also becoming more important in purchasing decisions, though price still remains pivotal among the majority of the population in most major markets.

Retailer loyalty schemes and associated bonuses and discounts are expected as the norm now. Never before has there been so much loyalty! Such schemes are becoming a cost the industry has to bear to protect its existing customer base and obtain the customer/consumer information it needs.

The shopper

Demographic changes are influencing shopper habits. The traditional family model where one parent works and the other stays at home to raise the family is increasingly rare. In more and more families both parents work and many single parents combine pursuing a career with raising children.

This makes traditional store opening patterns at best inconvenient, and for many families impossible. This is driving longer opening hours including 24-hour opening and Sunday trading in many markets. Efforts to resist this change have only been partially successful.

The markets

In mature markets such as the US, western Europe, Australasia and parts of the Pacific Rim opportunities for real volume growth are limited in many categories of fast-moving consumer goods. Retailers compete aggressively for market share on value-for-money, quality and convenience.

Planning restrictions make major new out-of-town store developments almost impossible in many such markets. This is driving the major multiple retailers back into the high street and encouraging them to try new retail formats. Retailers continue to squeeze manufacturers' prices to protect their own margins, while at the same time interest in more holistic category management approaches grows.

Manufacturers compete aggressively with one another, and with retailers' own label products, on brand values, quality and price. Product innovation is no longer just driven by the branded goods manufacturers as innovation becomes a greater part of retailer strategy.

> Product innovation is no longer just driven by the branded goods manufacturers as innovation becomes a greater part of retailer strategy

In spite of recent economic events, retailers and manufacturers see developing markets such as China, Latin America and central Europe as providing the major opportunities for growth. Major retailers are investing heavily in expansion into these markets, both through acquisition and new store building programmes. Manufacturers are similarly acquiring local producers and investing in major new production facilities in these markets.

Globalization

While the industry is becoming more and more responsive to individual consumer preferences and needs, it is also becoming increasingly global in nature. To realize economies of scale, manufacturing organizations are focusing production, distribution and sales/marketing to address market opportunities on a regional and global basis.

The retail sector is also awakening to the benefits of globalization, albeit with an emphasis to date on global retail branding, and to realizing the benefits of global purchasing power and harmonization of trading terms. As retailers globalize, there is a shift in the balance of power in their favour versus the manufacturing community and this has considerable implications for manufacturers in the way they support and serve such retailers.

One of the key drivers of manufacturer globalization is the need to address this increasing imbalance of power that they face with the retail sector. Manufacturer strategy therefore often revolves around building and exploiting the power of global brands to offset this.

Global communications, particularly via the new media, are creating new marketing opportunities for retailers and manufacturers on a one-to-one and a mass basis. On balance, the manufacturing sector is likely to benefit from such new developments in the nature and variety of channels to market which may increase consumer choice and reduce the dominance of the major multiple retailers.

Legislation

Legislation, while designed to protect the consumer, places increasing burdens on manufacturer and retailer costs and margins. New laws covering food hygiene, health and safety, enforcing the validity of advertising and promotional claims, and anti-monopoly legislation, are all designed to protect the interests of the consumer. The consumer products supply chain will also be effected by environmental legislation to reduce road traffic and minimize packaging wastage, and this may accelerate shifts to new channels to market.

Channels to market

With recent, dramatic advances in technology, there are now the beginnings of a likely upsurge in new channels to market, presenting considerably more choice for the consumer. The growing availability of Internet technology has meant an increase in web shopping, which will be further enhanced by the growth of interactive digital television.

Catalogue shopping has become more popular. Once restricted to the lower end of the market, this is moving more up-market, with many high street retailers expanding into this area. There has also been a growth in network marketing operations, which carry the advantage of very low set-up and infrastructure costs.

Opportunities in this area are particularly promising in emerging markets, as a very effective low-cost method of reaching consumers in countries where the infrastructure required for traditional retailing is lacking.

A proliferation in channels to market inevitably means a shift in the balance of power from retailer to manufacturer, where manufacturers are able to develop a one-to-one relationship with the end user for the first time. This brings huge opportunities to respond to customer needs and to tailor product and service offerings to their individual requirements.

Issues for retailers and manufacturers

Achieving profitable growth in mature markets is increasingly tough. Growth rates are low or non-existent, competition is fierce, consumers are becoming ever more demanding and the broadcast media that have traditionally been used to communicate with the consumer are becoming fragmented and more costly.

For leading retailers, especially in mainstream grocery, achieving profitable growth is becoming increasingly dependant on:

- **Their success as marketeers**. Leading retailers are beginning to make the transition to being true marketeers, able to approach the consumer with a powerful brand proposition.
- **Focus on the consumer and shopper**. Leading retailers are also investing heavily in getting closer to the customer, understanding better their preferences and needs, and in winning their loyalty.
- **Broadening their product and service portfolio**. Retailers are leveraging their brand strength and relationship with the consumer in offering new products and services to win a greater share of household expenditure.
- **Optimizing category performance**. A focus on category performance is increasingly seen to lie at the heart of optimizing total business performance and this in turn is driving organizational change, skills development and relationships with suppliers. A better understanding of the consumer and shopper and collaboration with strategic suppliers lies at the heart of improving category performance.
- **Developing new channels to market**. Demographic changes, enabling technology and competitive pressures are opening up direct communication with the consumer and new channels to market.
- **Harnessing technology in support of all the above**. Retailer decision-making is becoming increasingly sophisticated and data-rational as they invest in tools to capture, manage and exploit customer information. The resulting better understanding of consumer and shopper behaviours and preferences is driving both relationship marketing programmes and store design, ranging, merchandising and promotional activity.

Perhaps the greatest challenge of all facing major retail organizations is in changing mindsets to establish the new ways of working. The most advanced retailers are succeeding in making the change from traders to marketeers, in the early stages of this process often recruiting leading marketing professionals from outside the retail industry to develop and manage "the brand".

The same retailers are, however, sometimes struggling in changing their approach to working with manufacturers with whom relationships have historically been confrontational.

The leading multiple retailers are strong — and becoming stronger as they become more sophisticated — more integrated globally, and control greater market shares. For all but the very strongest fast-moving consumer goods manufacturers they present formidable and demanding customers.

The issues facing leading branded goods manufacturers are therefore driven by retailer strength, by competition with other manufacturers, and by the ever more demanding consumer and shopper.

Survival issues

Survival and profitable growth in this challenging environment is increasingly dependent on the following factors.

● **Building and maintaining strong consumer demand for strategic brands**. Strong brands remain the branded goods manufacturers' greatest asset. Directly, they provide strong demand for product and consequent profitable revenue streams. Indirectly, they make the manufacturer important to the retailer's business and ensure a continued high-profile presence in key retail channels to market. Understanding the consumer and retaining their brand loyalty is therefore vital.

● **Product innovation**. In mature markets almost all real profitable volume growth comes from successful new product development and introduction. Again, this depends on deep insights into consumer preferences and needs.

● **Focus on core categories**. The retailers' drive to optimize category performance is encouraging manufacturers to focus on the categories in which they have the strongest brands, resources and skills to excel in total category development. Manufacturers are exploiting this category of shopper and consumer behavioural understanding to reinforce their position as preferred suppliers to the retail trade.

● **Optimizing return on marketing investment**. Maintaining strong brands is expensive and the media is becoming more fragmented and more costly with media inflation running well ahead of retail price inflation in many major markets. With detailed information becoming available about individuals' consumers' and shoppers' response to media and trade promotion investment, manufacturers are, for the first time, able to evaluate objectively what works and what does not.

● **Harnessing technology**. Better understanding the consumer and shopper, optimizing return on market-

ing spend, and offering the retailer guidance on total category planning and management all require manufacturers to analyze and add value to large amounts of trading and other information. Technology therefore plays a key role in the new way of doing business.

● **Developing their organization and skills**. The new focus on understanding consumer and shopper behaviour and on using this learning to build a different kind of relationship with the retail trade requires dedicated, skilled category management resources and a new total business perspective. The most advanced manufacturers already have this in place and compete with one another for retailer attention.

Understanding the consumer and shopper to build brand loyalty increasingly lies therefore at the heart of retailer and manufacturer business strategies. Sharing this knowledge will provide the basis for future collaboration to optimize category performance to mutual commercial benefit. Exploiting this knowledge will also be the primary weapon in the forthcoming battle between retailer and manufacturer to own the customer's heart and wallet in the 21st century.

Better understanding the customer

In the consumer goods industry the word customer has to be used with considerable caution. One has consumers, shoppers, retailers, manufacturers, wholesalers, brokers and a variety of other participants in the end-to-end demand and supply chain. There are many supplier/customer relationships involved.

Understanding and meeting customer requirements is a key driver of success in the consumer goods manufacturing and retail sectors — perhaps more so than in any other sector today. To do this, the retailer needs an intimate knowledge of the shopper and consumer and this understanding is increasingly achievable.

Leading retailers are investing heavily in understanding their customers. Often this takes the form of loyalty card schemes that allow the retailer to combine geo-demographic information about an individual with detailed purchase transaction history. This information is used to drive marketing and promotional activity, monitor responses and continuously refine targeting to optimize payback on outbound communication programmes and in-store promotional investment.

For the manufacturer there is an added complication — while the need to know the customer necessitates in-depth understanding of the shopper and consumer, it also requires that they understand their trade partners — the retailers. Knowing one's trade partner means understanding their strategies, how they operate, the characteristics of the consumers and shoppers who form their target markets, and their objectives for the categories in which the manufacturer participates.

Just as retailers are becoming more sophisticated in their decision-making, so leading manufacturers are becoming increasingly analytical in the way they choose to invest in category partnership activities with leading retailers. Margin achieved, growth potential, attitude towards collaboration, profile of consumer base and a strategic assessment of future commercial success all play a role in deciding with which trade partner to invest precious skilled resources and funds.

Understanding the consumer and shopper, and sharing this knowledge, is the foundation for mutually profitable trading partnerships. However, against a background of the adversarial trading relationships common in the consumer goods sector, sharing detailed customer information is also still an area of considerable sensitivity. Given their common interest in the end consumer, manufacturers and retailers are beginning to address the challenges of customer information sharing in a more collaborative environment.

The advent of information technology is creating a proliferation of customer, consumer and shopper data. Both consumer products manufacturers and retailers face the challenge of separating core information from that which is nice to know, and to employ the appropriate technology enablers to store, manipulate and interrogate the data, and thus add value to decision-making. A clear customer information management strategy is key to this.

Segmentation and targeting

With recent developments in information technology, it will no longer be necessary to sample data about customers: the consumer goods industry is fast approaching a situation where it can collect data relating to every single individual customer, down to the individual transaction level. Retailers are just beginning to exploit the power of the data warehouses and databases underpinning their loyalty card schemes that make this possible. This will provide an understanding of the buying habits and preferences of individual customers, not just focus groups or survey samples.

For the first time, detailed information is therefore available about actual behaviour, as opposed to intended or expected buying behaviour. Traditional, static segmentation techniques such as ABC are becoming obsolete. One can now know the profiles of the shoppers that responded to a specific in-store promotion or product launch and in what store and even know at what time of the day different groups of shoppers visited the store and can fine-tune the merchandising accordingly. This is enormously valuable to consumer goods manufacturers and retailers in optimizing total category performance and in achieving a one-to-one relationship with the consumer.

Retailers are just beginning to exploit the power of the data warehouses and databases underpinning their loyalty card schemes that make this possible

The role of technology

Technology plays a key role in understanding the consumer and shopper and in targeting them with products and services that respond to their preferences and needs.

Advances in data warehousing mean companies are now able to store detailed information about individual customers and their purchasing patterns. More importantly, advanced data mining and data modelling techniques allow this data to be interpreted intelligently, making it possible to deliver increasingly sophisticated customer-centric offerings to the consumer and shopper.

Modelling techniques are used to create scenarios from the data, to test out the potential impact of particular marketing campaigns and to identify particularly profitable groups of customers which can then be targeted. These advantages are not just being realized in marketing to consumers, business-to-business marketing is also benefiting.

Technological developments are also enabling faster, more efficient, more reliable supply chain operations. Electronic data interchange (EDI) already allows retailer and manufacturer databases to be aligned and has made the ordering and replenishment process quicker, more accurate and more flexible.

New, Internet-based technology is also being used to share a much wider range of information about expected demand and supply. This allows joint planning between retailer and manufacturer and is making it possible to respond much more quickly to changing demand patterns. Other developments such as more intelligent bar-coding and electronic tagging provide for improved product traceability and monitoring of products from factory to checkout.

Technological developments are also affecting the front of the store to help customer service. The advent of self-scanning is reducing check-out queues, and thus lessens the main complaint of supermarket shoppers. The closer linkage of the retailer's consumer/shopper databases with operational store systems makes it possible to target tailored offers to the individual consumer at the point of sale — a strategy now being pursued by a number of leading retailers.

Kiosk shopping is potentially a key area for growth in the future, enabling the ordering of goods and services from convenient locations that fit in with consumer lifestyles. Kiosks also present opportunities for a two-way dialogue between retailer and consumer, with targeted promotional offers.

In summary, the quality of data available to support decision-making for both retailers and manufacturers has improved dramatically. The key is to utilize the tools and techniques available to maximum effect to support the new ways of doing business.

Exploiting technology for integrated marketing/in-store activity

There is a clear trend towards a more seamless marketing and trading environment and it is technology that is making this possible. For the retailer, data warehouses containing consumer, shopper and purchase transaction information, drive outbound marketing programmes that target individuals with the products and services that match most closely their interests and needs.

The same information will also drive the planning and management of product categories in-store — ensuring that product ranging, merchandising, price and availability fulfil consumer and shopper expectations and that the return on investment in marketing and promotional activities is optimized.

Increasingly, leading manufacturers are participating in this process and, in the most advanced markets, are competing actively for opportunities to work in collaboration with major retailers on overall category development. They are directly researching consumer and in-store shopper behaviour, sharing retailer category EPoS data, and applying analytical tools to model and optimize total category performance and provide planning recommendations to the retailer.

The benefits to the manufacturer for its core product categories of participation in the retailer's decision-making process for the category are considerable. It moves the dialogue away from price and margin towards joint business development and improves payback on investment with the trade partner. It also provides valuable insight into the consumer and shopper that aids new product development.

The benefits for the retailer are also considerable as skilled category-focused resources are made available by the manufacturer free of change.

In the most advanced markets, the impact of such an application of technology is having a major impact on consumer goods retailing and manufacturers business models.

The new approach to doing business requires a shared vision and teamwork across different functions in the business — commercial, operational and financial, and between retailer and manufacturer. The advent of efficient consumer response (ECR) and category management are acting as catalysts for this development and provide a joint focus on the most efficient way of meeting and exceeding consumer requirements.

Such a realignment implies the need for a radical reappraisal of traditional organization structures, processes and information flows. Capturing learning and using knowledge effectively is also becoming a core skill, which all companies must learn and develop if they are to succeed in this environment.

Chapter 8: Financial services

Overview

Customer demands and competitive threats are forcing traditional financial services companies to rethink their business. Their conclusion is that technology matters — but that it does not run the show. In the customer revolution, both customers and the business should be involved in shaping the technology support.

The retail financial services executive today needs to know what is possible, what works on scale, and most importantly, what customers value. They can then invest in the right areas to optimize accessibility, convenience, loyalty and profit.

The tools and skills are available to make a retail financial services organization truly customer-focused. However, the wide variability in profitability of different customer segments is not consistent with the traditional practice of undifferentiated products pricing and service. The desire to embark or, if started, accelerate along the course of becoming customer-focused is in the organization's hands.

Hard decisions will need to be made and followed through, while tight programme management including the realization of the benefits is fundamental. It is relatively easy to buy the underlying technology — the hard part will be re-designing the entire customer management process to ensure the organization is focusing on the customer.

Some companies will do nothing — and their demise will not be far away.

Others will make use of the technology but will not have aligned the organization to take advantage of it, and as a result will produce mixed results. The successful retail financial services companies of the future will embrace the challenge, configure their processes around the customer, redesign the infrastructure and support the strategy with appropriate technology. Then they will have focused on their customers.

Challenges facing financial services

The challenges facing the financial services industry include globalization, diversification and the need for customer focus.

Globalization

Being big in financial services nowadays is not about bricks and mortar. New market entrants, both foreign and start-up, are predominantly "virtual" — using the latest technology and they are catching ill-prepared incumbents on the hop.

Financial service providers in the UK are facing both domestic and foreign competition. National supermarket chains have entered the retail banking and savings market, while both UK startups like Virgin and well established US organizations are using call centres and the Internet to attract customers. American credit card companies such as MBNA, Advanta and Capital One have been successful in penetrating the UK market and have surprised the domestic companies which had believed the market was theirs alone.

Diversification

The situation is becoming more and more competitive as organizations move into areas outside their previous sphere of operations. Major shifts here have been:

● Retail banks and building societies are becoming bancassurers through the offer of mostly tied (own brand) regulated products;

● Insurance companies are offering banking services — such as Standard Life Bank, part of Europe's largest mutual insurance company, which is launching the nine-minute mortgage;

● Investment banks are offering smaller end investment products such as unit

trusts (mutual funds) through direct channels — the US has a mutual fund industry that is marginally larger than its banking system; and

● New entrants such as Virgin, Security First Network Bank (the first full-service Internet bank) and retailers such as Marks and Spencer, Sainsbury and Tesco in the UK are offering insurance and banking products.

In addition, the traditional providers are now using non-traditional channels such as the Internet, kiosks and supermarkets.

Customer focus

Established players in all national markets know that they need to change their business plans from being product-focused to being customer-focused. Recognizing this, however, is a long way from achieving it.

The process of moving to a customer-oriented approach can be difficult. Decision support tools need to be used to identify the most profitable customers and to target them with bespoke products. To offer bespoke services cost-effectively means taking full advantage of sales force automation and customer relationship management technologies. Competitive prices and service levels have to match not just the other banks but the best consumer-facing companies.

The market place has changed. There is a new order in which barriers to entry are few and new, lithe entrants providing differentiated products and services by segment can more than ably compete. Customers are shopping around, demanding greater convenience and are less complacent or apathetic than they used to be.

Many incumbents believe they already focus on their customers. If that is the case they should be easily able to respond to the following five questions.

● How many customers do they have, not counting duplicates?
● Who are their profitable customers?
● Are costs allocated in a way which reveals net profitability?
● What is the lifetime value of each customer?
● Are there different treatment strategies for different customers?

It is only when an organization knows the answers to these questions that it can begin to tailor its response. Technology enables the organization to answer the questions and deliver that tailored response.

Applying the technology
Knowing the customer

Financial services organizations have enough data on their customers to effect a sea-change in the way they manage the relationship. Lack of data is not a problem. The challenges are raising the quality of the data, then storing and accessing it. The ability to effectively draw knowledge and insights from that data to support relationship management is elusive.

With research showing that the cost of acquiring a customer is increasing, the fact that financial service organizations lose 50% of their customers every five years indicates there is a hole to be plugged. To do so means that they must:

● provide excellent customer service whenever the customer contacts the organization;
● create a relationship with the customer to lengthen the life of the relationship, and thereby reduce the acquisition costs associated with replacing lost customers;
● develop profitable and attractive product and service propositions; and,
● know which products and services a customer will purchase next by understanding at what stage they have reached in their lives — and then embark upon highly targeted marketing campaigns.

Segmentation

Why segment? It has been shown that groups of customers behave in similar ways, and so it makes sense to treat such groups in a similar fashion. But there is a cost to segmentation. Segments are dynamic, not static. The way a segment behaved yesterday may change tomorrow, with half the segment behaving in an unexpected way.

Segmentation techniques can now accommodate the most sophisticated of criteria. Companies that exploit this technique can gain market share in mature markets through the use of tools to analyze the influence of geo-demographics, psychographics, behaviour and life cycle.

The art of segmentation is continually evolving with the increased use of data mining/business intelligence and techniques such as fractal analysis. There are many providers that will take a customer database and segment it according to externally derived parameters, often on a monthly basis. This first cut can then be manipulated with the financial services organization's segmentation criteria.

It is now generally accepted that not all wealthy customers are profitable and, as such, segmentation techniques are being used first to understand who the profitable customers are and then to enable dynamic targeting. Once the organization understands how its customers are grouped at that point in time, it can target customers of that group who do not yet hold the predicted basket of products, bearing in mind that there is an optimum number of products held beyond which customer profitability reduces.

Micro-segmentation and targeting can then be used to prove a hypothesis such as a segment's propensity for the next purchase. With this knowledge the retail financial services provider can deploy marketing spend more effectively.

Maintaining the relationship

Financial services companies are keen to show their customers the extent of their relationship with them. A lot of energy has been expended around the creation of the single customer view, but it is a situation that eludes most major financial services organizations that are battling with data protection legislation and numerous legacy systems.

Improved use of the standard statement, or passbook, is being adopted by many financial services companies. Citibank recently introduced its new format statements which include details of the customer's current, savings, loan accounts, credit cards and investments all in the one document. Statements now include, personalized messages on how the customer can best manage their financial affairs based on what Citibank knows about their financial details.

Insurance companies probably have an even steeper hill to climb as, historically, these organizations were a collection of different product companies with separate systems, customer databases, marketing functions, technology architecture and infrastructure. With the move to cross- product selling and now the launch of many direct banking operations, a single customer view is critical to establishing a solid relationship with the customer.

Customer profitability

Diagrams like the one below show what many suspect — that some customers are not pulling their weight.

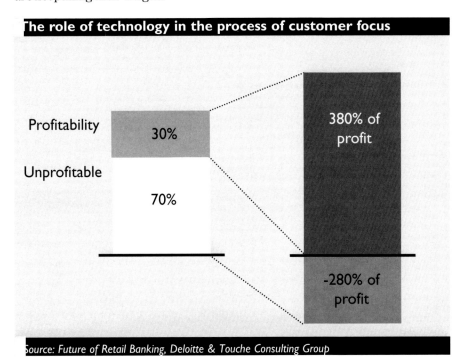

The role of technology in the process of customer focus

Profitability — 30%

380% of profit

Unprofitable — 70%

-280% of profit

Source: Future of Retail Banking, Deloitte & Touche Consulting Group

Understanding the profitability by each customer's usage of its products and services avoids problems such as the one many banks face, for example, when customers do not close their accounts but leave them ticking over. If the customer moves to another bank to deposit the bulk of the money but use the previous account for standing orders and direct debits the account is theoretically not lost — a small balance is maintained — but its profitability is minimal.

Salesforce automation

Investment fund brokers such as Charles Schwab in the US have embraced sophisticated sales force automation software and increased their business — offering more than execution only but at a fraction of the cost of more traditional stock brokers. Such automated telephone servicing and selling is a core plank of their strategy for servicing customers.

Call centres

Call centres cut account handling costs (the costs of a local branch network) and they generate income by selling financial products. Representatives are trained on how to identify selling opportunities from a relationship profile during the actual telephone conversation with the customer. Software also exists to prompt representatives to suggest appropriate selling opportunities during each call.

Call centres are a core part of any retail financial services organization's channel strategy — a strategy that must focus on the customer. Using technology, leading organizations will quickly integrate the call centres into the service offering by capitalizing on changing customer preferences, such as the desire to buy commodity products over the telephone.

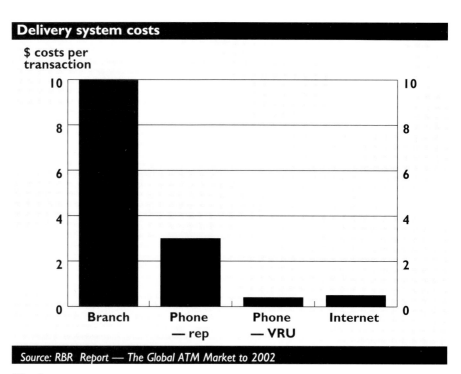

Delivery system costs

Source: RBR Report — The Global ATM Market to 2002

The Internet

There has been considerable media attention focused on the importance of the Internet in the marketplace of the future. However, retail financial services executives are still attempting to assess the potential of on-line delivery.

PC banking has not been taken up in large numbers: of Barclays' 10 million customers, only a small percentage, about 0.4%, have signed up for PC banking following its launch in early 1997.

Banks have seen the Internet as an alternative delivery channel, but not one that replaces traditional forms of contact with the customers.

If the demand for on-line banking matches the predictions, bankers need to act now. US providers such as Security First Network Bank lead the pack but even they are not yet able to offer an international service.

In contrast to retail banking, the use of the Internet in US securities firms is relatively advanced. According to a December 1997 Tower Group survey, 62% of large US securities firms offered Internet trading. The survey also found that US securities firms are planning to increase their Internet spending five-fold over the next three years, resulting in 10 million Internet trading accounts by 2001.

The introduction of Internet trading has led to a variety of strategic responses. Internet brokers like E*Trade and AmeriTrade provide execution of trades at a fraction of the cost charged by a traditional, full-service broker. In contrast, full-service firms like Merrill Lynch charge much higher commissions but provide customized financial planning and research through their brokers.

Some firms are mixing these approaches, blurring the distinction between full-service and discount brokerage. For example, Charles Schwab provides on-line trades at a discount but also provides the advice and research usually associated only with full-service brokers. Morgan Stanley Dean Witter offers both full-service brokerage services as well as low-cost execution of trades over the Internet through Discover. Although pursuing quite different strategies, all these firms have been successful.

Insurance executives are enthusiastic about the potential of selling over the Internet. At the moment, the Internet is principally a communication tool for insurers, but several companies are building transactional Web sites and entering into technology partnerships

There are obstacles. Surveys have found that the most common reason cited for resistance to purchasing insurance products on-line is the need for more personal attention. Consumers of insurance products appear concerned that their individual needs will not be met as fully using the Internet compared to using an agent.

Integration of delivery channels

The integration of delivery channels will optimize the customer interaction. Research has shown that customers will use a variety of channels depending on the nature of that interaction.

Channel integration

Branches	Sales	Service	Transaction	Leveraged links
Full service	●	●	●	✓
Convenience banking centres	●	●	●	✓
ATMs				
Traditional	●	○	●	
Enhanced	●	●	●	
Call centre (manned)				
Customer Service	○	●	○	
7/24 Bank	●	●	●	✓
Out-bound telemarketing	●	●	●	✓
Electronic banking				
PC home banking	○	●	●	
VRU home banking				
PC bill payment				
Internet banking	○	●	●	
Direct mail	○	●	○	✓

Key: ○ High fit ● Low fit

Source: McKinsey & Co

Understanding what channels are best suited for each type of transaction for each customer allows the offerings to be configured to optimize the service for the customer while ensuring that the bank's costs are covered. Branch and round-the-clock call centre channels meet the three basic requirements of sales, service and advice, and transaction.

Many professionals are increasingly optimistic about the scope for interaction. "We believe our future customers will require an anytime, anywhere access framework which supports any communications medium, voice, e-mail, fax and ultimately video," says David Travers of USAA, a major US insurance company.

An integrated delivery channel offering as described by Travers requires a single view of the customer and consistency of service, otherwise it becomes simply a proliferation of delivery channels rather than an integrated offering.

To support such a structure the organization will require real-time collection and dissemination of appropriate information to all the delivery channels. This ensures the customers perceive just one relationship with the organization, rather than many relationships depending upon which delivery channel they access.

Another requirement is for common standards of security. The financial institution that does not require its customers to have more than one PIN to access the full range of products will have differentiated itself in that major customer desire for convenience.

Retail financial services organizations are beginning to promote different uses of different channels, although there is little evidence of a channel-wide strategic approach. Abbey National has introduced a service charge for customers of certain accounts to deter them from using the branch. Comerica, a US retail bank, promotes branchless banking with improved lending and savings rates in exchange for customer commitments not to visit branches and only use the remote channels. In the UK, building societies have for some time offered postal savings accounts which offer better interest rates but all contact is by post or telephone.

In practice, many UK retail financial services companies are hedging their bets — investing a modest portion of their budgets in a variety of channels until customer preferences become clear. It is a position of reacting to the customer, rather than leading their behaviour.

Chapter 9: Public sector

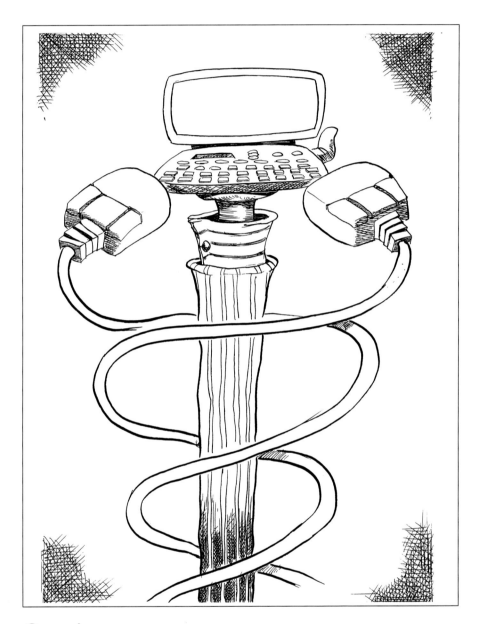

Overview

The effort to create more customer-focused government agencies and public services is turning into a drive towards direct access; encouraging customers to use new channels to obtain the information and services they need. Better customer relationship management is also being facilitated by the recognition, among segments of the public sector, of the need to share information more effectively between different agencies.

Several new technologies are enabling people to get support from public organizations more quickly. Call centres, kiosks, the Internet and-smart cards are examples of these technologies. The considerations associated with implementing these technologies, and the value to be derived from them, vary across technologies and across public organizations.

The most immediate impact of direct access services is the ability to serve a larger number of customers, but there are some impacts that will take longer to be fully realized. The absence of human interface suggests an increase in the standardization of service delivery.

For the most part, the standardization is acceptable, but inevitably there will be cases that should have received special handling and did not. The greater reliance on technology may also help portions of the population, who would have otherwise not been exposed to new technology, become more proficient in the use of such technology.

As technology enables agencies to work more closely together and to package services to individuals, communities will hopefully see an increase in the effectiveness of those services. However, agencies will need to become more technologically sophisticated to guard against increased fraud and the abuse of government systems. Privacy issues will also continue to arise, as more information about individuals becomes widely available, shared among agencies, and subject to computer hacking.

Within public agencies, many will face changes in how staff resources are assigned, processes are performed and jobs designed, the skills required by both service and technology staff, and even their physical environments.

Agencies may become more likely to seek a technological solution to increases in demand for services, rather than increase in labour budgets. They may also use technology projects as an opportunity to redesign their services and products. As agencies implement the new technologies, they may be able to better collect data that helps them assess their performance and profile customers.

In summary, the desired impact of technology-enabled direct access services is dependent on the ability to deliver more and better targeted services to the public.

The challenge

In the face of constant public spending cuts, most government organizations want to take advantage of new technologies to achieve their work more cost-effectively. This move extends beyond using technology to cut internal costs. It already embraces a desire to have the customer interact and receive services through automated systems.

Some of the movement towards direct access services has occurred in conjunction with major systems conversions or enhancements driven by Year 2000 requirements. Because of Year 2000 concerns, many organizations that might have had other priorities are assessing and investing in their technology infrastructures. Organizations that must change their technology environments to be Year 2000 compliant are frequently maximizing their return on investment in new technology by improving the functionality of their systems and even fundamentally changing the way they conduct business.

Unfortunately, Year 2000 investments do not always result in improved service delivery. Some organizations are putting substantial resources towards patching ineffective, inefficient systems that serve neither the agencies nor the public well.

Several other technology trends are encouraging the deployment of direct access services. Many citizens prefer self-service technologies because they offer them flexibility in the location and time at which they receive services and they are often quicker than traditional service delivery modes. While the prolific sharing of information has made some people reluctant to provide personal information, it has also made them more interested in forms of interaction that allow them to maintain some privacy or anonymity.

Growing use of the Internet and the advances in computing and telecommunication power of recent years have made it more practical for agencies to push data gathering and reporting to geographically dispersed locations, thereby making it more cost-effective for them to reach their customers.

Other forces have also been steering public agencies towards direct access services for many years. For several years, movements to reduce the burden on taxpayers have limited the growth of public budgets. At the same time, public expectations regarding the volume and quality of publicly provided services have increased.

The need to do more with less has led many agencies to search for ways of providing services that are less labour-intensive, that reduce redundancies, and that make the customer an active participant in the provision of services. Many of these approaches to innovation were also promoted by popular concepts such as Total Quality Management and Business Process Reengineering.

Sociologists have long proposed that social problems are strongly interlinked and that a person with one problem is very likely to have several others. In some countries, such as the US, a consolidation or agglomeration of services has been taking place as traditionally separate agencies try to work together.

As agencies try to implement the concept of one-stop shopping they often seek a common customer interface that is widely accessible and that then routes the information to either a shared database or different databases maintained by separate organizations. This allows them to make service provision decisions based on data that is consistent across organizations.

> New technologies allow the provision of routine services to occur throughout the day, reducing the volume of requests — and therefore the backlog — during normal business hours

The movement towards government direct access services is not marked by any watershed event. Instead it has been the natural result of several separate trends in government and technology and is still increasing in its use and acceptance world-wide.

From schools, hospitals and libraries to large national agencies, government organizations are learning that technologies such as voice response systems, the Internet, smart cards and call centres can:

- improve the ability to serve more customers;
- achieve greater consistency, currency, and accuracy of information; and,
- better allocate resources

Serving customers better

Because customers are able to access services remotely and at virtually the moment they need them, they spend less time in getting to the office where the service used to be delivered. New technologies also allow the provision of routine services to occur throughout the day, reducing the volume of requests — and therefore the backlog — during normal business hours. As resources are better allocated, customers are more quickly directed towards the service provider that can most rapidly and appropriately serve them.

For example, because individuals can get information they need from the Internet, at a kiosk, or from a recorded message, there are fewer such basic requests made directly to agency staff. Because customers can access these technologies potentially around the clock and because the number of customers who can be served by such technology simultaneously is very high, the number of customers with basic requests that can be served can grow exponentially.

As those customer needs are met more quickly and for an increased number of individuals, the agency is also better able to apply its human resources to meeting the more complex needs of customers.

In addition to the improved logistics, direct access services may encourage individuals, who would have otherwise been reluctant to request support, to access those services. Greater privacy, convenience of access, or simply a new awareness of those services will encourage them. The real benefit here is in reaching individuals who, otherwise, may have never been served at all.

Gaining better quality information

Where data is collected at a single point of contact with a customer and immediately shared among several databases/service providers, it is more likely that the agencies using that data will be operating on consistent and current information. If multiple data entry of the same information across agencies is reduced or eliminated, the agencies can expect a reduction in the number of data entry errors, as well.

To the extent that a direct service technology enables customers to input information about themselves directly, data entry errors are likely to be reduced. The time spent by the public and public agencies in correcting those errors would also be reduced, as would the period during which service is not provided or inappropriately provided.

However, there is some risk that untrained individuals will not understand how to enter data or will deliberately enter erroneous data.

Better allocation of resources

Because several of the technologies support a mix of customers, agencies are able to allocate resources cost-effectively. They may respond to routine requests with automated support or through staff with limited training or experience. This allows the more experienced staff to focus on more complex services. It can also reduce the number of staff required to respond to customer requests.

The technologies needed

The variety of technologies that can be employed and the different benefits that can be derived from them are enticing. However, the investment of time and resources that some technologies require, the challenges of acquiring and retaining staff with the requisite knowledge and skills in current technology, and the potential complexity associated with major implementations can be overwhelming.

Not surprisingly, the public agencies that are most successful in employing direct access services are those that invest time and resources in recognizing and addressing the factors and issues that are key to their specific environments.

Call centres

Call centre technology routes inbound calls so that resources can be allocated to the different customer needs. They also enable organizations to mix the reception of calls efficiently with the placing of calls to customers so that the productivity of telephone agents is maximized. New developments in this technology automatically provide on-line customer information to the agent speaking with a customer.

A common limitation of many call centres is that they still do not put data entry into the hands of the customer. Time and human resources are still spent receiving data from the customer and entering it into the organization's information system.

Organizations whose customers may need very different levels of service — or who update or provide information about customer cases primarily through the telephone — may find this technology particularly useful.

Public agencies such as those managing tax collection, benefits distribution, or immigration are also likely candidates.

Kiosks

This technology allows individuals to access a moderate amount of information and in some cases, to record a small amount of information, at a convenient location. The key advantage of kiosks is that they can be placed in locations with high potential customer traffic. Customers do not need to have purchased any personal technology such as a personal computer.

The major disadvantage is that kiosks are limited in the amount of information they can manage. Currently they are more useful for presenting information than for collecting and processing it, but the possibilities for sophisticated identification and interaction do exist (for example, check-ins and alcohol consumption tests for people on parole).

In the public sector, kiosks have been used by agencies whose potential customers are varied and geographically dispersed, and whose service needs require relatively limited information. Agencies providing travel and tourism information have used kiosks to present local bus service schedules and national parks information. These are excellent examples of how direct access services get public service information to those who need it, when and where they need it.

They also present a great opportunity to limit the costs of keeping public information current. The number of required brochures can be reduced and updates can be made less expensively and distributed more quickly. Kiosks have also been used to process driver's licence and vehicle registration information, and to list local job openings.

Interactive voice response (IVR)

At its most basic level, IVR is a relatively inexpensive technology that can be easily implemented by most organizations. Organizations can use it to direct callers towards recorded messages that provide them with answers to frequently asked questions. That frees staff to handle more complex calls and to perform other work.

IVR technology can be combined with other telecommunications technologies to increase the complexity of service provided through a telephone call.

At a basic level, IVR technology is widely used by public agencies that receive many common, simple telephone queries.

Internet/intranet services

As use and acceptance of the Internet spreads, public agencies are finding that it can be a cost-effective mechanism for informing and serving customers. This technology clearly depends upon customers having access to a computer and the Internet. Nowadays it is increasingly common to have such access or for communities to provide accessibility as a public service such as through local libraries. Agencies are able to provide information about themselves and the services they provide. As with IVRs, the Internet frees staff to spend their time addressing more complex customer needs.

The Internet can do more than serve as a bulletin board or poster for an organization, but the value of even that simple support should not be underestimated. Web search engines can help individuals who are completely unaware of an agency's existence identify that agency as a source of assistance. This helps agencies target the dissemination of information to those individuals who are most likely to need that information.

More advanced Internet services include the dissemination of documents, for example, tax reporting forms and databases (for, say, job announcements), the receipt of requests for additional information, receipt of enrolment information, purchases, and payments.

An intranet offers an agency the information dissemination and accessibility power of the Internet with the ability to control access to sensitive information. The key is the use of internal web servers through which the agency controls access to information. The value of an intranet in direct access services is indirect. It provides a common venue for accessing and exchanging sensitive information among agency colleagues, which can ultimately enable them to make more current and consistent information available to the public.

Smart cards

Smart cards have an embedded computer chip — either a microprocessor or a non-programmable memory chip. Computer activity occurs through contact with a smart card reader, reception of an electromagnetic signal, or, more recently, through a combination of contact and signal. The memory in smart cards allows reading/writing of information from and to the memory chip. They are more reliable and hold much more information than magnetic strip cards. The microprocessor smart cards can manipulate data in addition to receiving, storing, and transmitting data.

Because of their power and flexibility, smart cards offer a variety of uses, but they are most commonly used to provide access to pay phones. Europe is the leader in the use of smart cards although Asia and North America will increase their use of smart cards substantially over the next few years.

Cards that do not require contact are particularly useful when anything more time-consuming would disrupt throughput or affect safety. A primary example of that would be the collection of tolls electronically. Another major public sector application of smart cards is the provision and tracking of national health insurance as has been implemented in Germany. Other applications can be found in mass transit, passports, and licences.

Current developments in smart card technology include an open card that provides inter-operability of smart card applications across different types of computers. An emerging technology, Ibuttons, provides the functionality of smart cards on a ring that can be worn like jewellery, and the ring is even easier to use than contactless smart cards.

Systems integration/data sharing

One of the main historical impediments to co-ordination or consolidation of government services has been the separate system infrastructures and databases maintained by separately commissioned and funded organizations. This was especially true in the US, where federal funding from separate agencies was distributed to many different state and local government agencies for service delivery.

While the resistance to sharing a common database and control still exists, technology has made it easier for organizations to work towards a true one-stop delivery of government services. Agencies that may have political, cultural, data, or technology concerns, can ease into a closer working relationship by first sharing a common front end through which they interface with the public.

At this point they start to become comfortable with working together. They are also beginning to develop common terminology and an understanding of how they all serve the customer. Then integration of systems progresses with the targeting of those systems most receptive to integration — those where political and technical concerns are minimal. By allowing themselves more time to prepare and adjust to the changes and costs associated with systems integration, public agencies are becoming more successful with large projects to provide the public with a direct, one-stop service.

Even where they continue to maintain separate systems, the common interface facilitates sharing of data and co-ordination in the delivery of services. The State of Indiana provides an example of such a project. It has recently taken the first steps in a long-term project to bring together its state programmes for the unemployed.

> While the resistance to sharing a common database and control still exists, technology has made it easier for organizations to work towards a true one-stop delivery of government services

Internal challenges in deploying direct access services

The cost of direct service-enabling technology may be relatively inexpensive (as in the case of a simple IVR). But where the implementation of technology is complex, costs can mount very quickly.

Major cost components can include the following:
- hardware;
- software;
- communications infrastructure;
- experienced project managers;
- skilled designers, developers, and implementers;
- the time of in-house subject matter experts and management;
- experts in process redesign, job design, organizational design, and change management;
- training for, or hiring of, skilled technology staff;
- changes to facilities; and,
- long-term maintenance.

Because public agencies are subject to changes in their elected or appointed leadership, it can be difficult to get the commitment of funding and support for large, long-term efforts. Also, because many public organizations have not historically been able to update their technical environments, they often lack the technical infrastructure and expertise needed to adequately support and utilize new technologies.

Retaining skilled, experience technology staff is an additional challenge. Because public agencies must operate under public scrutiny, the media, and funding organizations, these agencies often find it very difficult to take risks or make substantial changes. Internally, agencies may also face resistance from employees who believe their job security is threatened. At the very least, agencies must often progress with change at a very slow pace and with much consideration of the concerns of its many stakeholders.

External challenges

The technical proficiency of the average consumer has increased over the past few decades, particularly in developed countries. Educational systems and a more general exposure to technology are making it more accepted and even desired. However, the proficiency of many of the target customers of government services is generally much lower than that of the population as a whole.

It may take another two decades for the vast majority of the population to be technically proficient enough to use self-service technology, and there will probably always remain a portion of the population that is resistant to or uneducated about such technology. Unfortunately, much of the population that is left behind will include people who would benefit from government services.

Similarly, the access to technologies such as the Internet has grown rapidly, as more people own personal computers and the number of Internet service providers increases. Still, many people, particularly low-income populations, are less likely to have access to computers or the Internet. Public agencies, such as libraries, have helped the situation by making computers and access to the Internet available to their communities.

One of the attractions of direct access services for the public may be the relative privacy within which they can request services. Associated with that benefit are some risks that agencies must recognize and address. For example, the remote technologies may make it easier for individuals to cheat — provide false information or have someone else pretend to be them. Services facing such risks include drivers' licence renewals, vehicle registrations, and parolee check-ins. The risks also exist with traditional modes of service delivery but to a lesser extent.

Because direct service technology can open an agency to a much larger number of individuals who can repeatedly access its systems very quickly, individuals can overload the system simply by submitting large numbers of requests. Organizations using the Internet risk unauthorized access and tampering — even of sensitive data that is not generally accessible on the Internet.

In making the decision to implement direct service technology, project champions and agency executives must make sure they have fully understood the risks and requirements associated with such endeavours.

They must also be committed to an investment of time, money, staff resources, and executive attention. For the simpler technologies, this may not be a hard commitment to make. For the more complex and far-reaching technologies, the commitment will be substantial.

Chapter 10: Telecoms

Overview

The telecoms industry continues to grow at an extraordinary rate. In western Europe alone the number of mobile phone subscribers has quadrupled from 15 million in 1994 to nearly 60 million at the beginning of 1998.

Customer demand over the last five years has led to massive investments in telecoms infrastructure that will only be profitable if telecoms operators can hold on to their high value customers. They have to protect and increase the revenues from these customers in a highly competitive and uncertain environment.

Telecoms businesses are already sophisticated in their use of technology in terms of infrastructure and products. However, they now need to use the customer-facing technologies of call centres, customer relationship management systems, saleforce automation, loyalty schemes and e-commerce to maintain communication with these profitable customers at acceptable cost.

Challenges ahead

The telecoms industry faces vast challenges in a host of different ways. It is no longer a homogenous utility — in the last decade it has changed beyond recognition. It comprises equipment manufacturers (switches, handsets, cable and infrastructure) and service providers and retailers as well as the traditional telcos, cable companies of fixed and wireless network operators and consumer retailers.

And with this change in structure and growing diversity of consumers, the telecoms industry is now having to reinvent itself again to go forward — to focus on the customers, at all levels.

Problem areas

The telecoms industry is experiencing vast changes — both social and technological — which throw up their own difficulties. The main problem areas are:

● **Rapidly changing customer demands**. Customer expectations increase. The expensive fixed communications links in use 10 years ago have given way to more flexible virtual private networks. Absolute reliability and excellent customer service are prerequisites. The customer is at last setting the pace.

● **Accelerating pace of technological advances**. Everybody knows that technology will keep advancing. The problem is predicting in which directions. Some predicted advances have not happened. So, for example, the delay in providing greater bandwidth over copper cable has allowed wireless and satellite technology to catch up.

> The telecoms industry is experiencing vast changes — both social and technological — which throw up their own difficulties

● **Shorter new service development/deployment cycles**. The lifecycle for developing and launching a service has gone down from years to months. Competitive pressure is forcing telecoms businesses to renew their ranges of products and services more often. They also have to deal with the long tail of customers that are using old products and services.

● **Less control over balancing network capacity/demand**. Forecasting demand for network capacity is more of an art than a science. Competition means that network providers find it difficult to use price to influence capacity. They are therefore spending large amounts of money on infrastructure to avoid being caught out.

● **Convergence of markets, industries, and technologies**. The digital age brings voice and data together. It has happened more slowly than expected, but recent technologies such as voice-over-web remove the traditional distinction between voice and data traffic. In the marketplace, the consumer is moving towards the same expectation of a 24-hour service from all their service providers — for a mobile telephone, a bank and for catalogue retailers.

● **Increasing politicization of regulatory decisions**. Some countries and regions have adopted a free market approach. Most continue to impose restrictions on telecoms activity under the guise of social or economic policy. Decisions are not just market-driven but have to be regulator-compliant.

The rule of three

Dealing with these difficulties will be a challenge. Industry predictions suggest that only the largest players will survive. The large incumbents at the beginning of the new millennium such as AT&T, Ericsson, Nokia, Sprint and Worldcom will still be there in five years' time, while the smaller players will fail to flourish.

A new rule has emerged in regional and increasingly in global markets, which applies among others to the telecoms industry. It states that: "A mature, stable market is dominated by three leaders".

The characteristics of the marketplace are that:

● Each of these inner circle players holds a 10% to 40% share;

● Together the big three control 70% to 90% of the market;

● A share of over 10% share is essential due to the cost of research and development, marketing, systems and overheads; and,

● Other participants will be specialists and niche players with 1% to 5% of the market.

A good example of this is in the long-distance call provision in the US. The market leaders are AT&T, MCI and Sprint. There are a large number of other smaller players.

Pinpointing the customer

However, being big or being a specialist may not be enough. As long ago as 1986, British Telecom was experimenting with one-to-one direct marketing. The technology in customer information management systems has moved on tremendously since then, so today the consumer is offered the choice of tailored tariffs, discounts and incentives. Frequently used numbers that attract discounts can be changed by the consumer via a touch-tone telephone call or by visiting the web site. Telephone bills show a wealth of detail (still complicated in places) which was absent 10 years ago.

Despite the size of many of the main industry players, there is a recognition that the companies that will be successful in the next 10 years are those that have pinpointed a few market segments. The companies which have a generalist approach will be overshadowed. The overriding strategy will be to do something very well.

There is a corresponding interest in customer segmentation. Part of this has been driven by the negative desire to reduce churn or turnover of customers. As the churn issue recedes, the greater interest in the customer is being driven by the economics of maintaining growth and profitability in a maturing market, where the average revenue per customer is declining.

Telecoms companies can no longer afford to use a mass-market approach to selling a product or service to the large percentage of nil profit customers.

The table below describes a typical coarse segmentation used to decide on the standard of service to different mobile user segments.

Service requirements for mobile user segments						
Segment	Sales channel	Air time	Handset cost	Appplication	Service standard	Churn critical
Emergency use	Retail	Low	Low	Voice	Low	Low
Lifestyle	Retail	Low	High	Voice	Low	High
Casual	Retail	Medium	Medium	Voice	Medium	Medium
Small business	Retail	High	Medium	Voice	High	High
Remote workers	Retail/ corporate	High	Medium	Voice, data, new services	High	HIgh
Business critical	Corporate	High	High	Data, voice, new services	High	High

Dealing with residential customers

Providing a high level of customer service to the swelling number of inexperienced as well as experienced customers is tricky. Call centres are swamped. Customer information systems are stretched. But, given time, inexperienced telecoms customers will become more educated and will expect a high level of service, just as they do in other areas of life.

So what are telecoms businesses doing to improve the way they deal with the well educated customer? Typically, they are giving their customers more control. They are improving their supply chain and administrative processes to eliminate delays. They are planning and targeting their promotions more carefully, using a mixture of mass market advertising (billboards, TV and radio) and micro-market advertising (direct mail, web marketing).

There is a convergence here with what other industries are doing, as best practices are transferred from one industry to another.

Dealing with the business customer

The majority of traffic passing over the world's networks is business usage — the telecoms industry provides services to every other industry. The demand from these other industries for telecommunications transport and value-added services will grow tremendously. These services are vital enablers to service businesses' efforts to reach and lock in high-value customers.

The scope of customer care operations that telecoms providers must support will be staggering. More than 300 million telephone calls will be completed every hour by 2000. Over the next 15 years, 800 million new phone lines should be installed world-wide, and more than 1.3 billion wireless phones will be deployed. The growth in requirements for data transmission eclipses even these requirements.

To deal with this, the telecoms industry will rely in even greater use of automation to handle sales and support processes.

Technologies employed

The telecoms industry is more aware of technology than many others. The list below describes some technologies that are being used now.

- **Videophone**. Face-to-face communication between business partners, also using technology to tie in customers and suppliers.
- **Call centre automation**. Fast, accurate fulfilment for simple information requests. Interactive voice response (IVR) allows the call to be handled without waiting for a customer service representative.
- **Web, call centre integration**. A customer starts to place an order via the web but needs assistance. If they hit the help button on the web page they are connected to an agent who is looking at the same web page as the caller. The agent helps the customer finish placing the order.

Applications required are: integration of automatic call distributor (ACD), customer advocacy automation software, Internet telephony gateways, web/server and electronic commerce solutions.

Use a mobile telephone in its simplest mode — dial the number, press the Connect button, speak and press the stop button — and you need little in the way of customer assistance. Managing a three-way telephone call is trickier, and the user who attempts wireless data transmission is likely to have to call the helpline.

Even data transmission via modems and fixed wire causes problems, like modems mysteriously failing to connect 100% of the time. Complexity in the telecoms industry is not easy to hide.

As in other industries, a picture of the customer's purchasing behaviour and contact history will build up over time. This data is stored in back office databases and can be accessed as part of the front office customer relationship Management (CRM) system used by the telecoms business. It can also be analyzed to feed back into segmentation and product development.

CRM packages are enabling increased customer contact, improved lead generation, and better service tracking as well as the ability to integrate all of these functions for greater customer management. While incumbent telecoms providers were early adopters of software that allowed them to capture data on customers, much of this was done on a product or geographic location basis.

It has only been in recent years that telecoms providers have begun to realize the power of developing and acting on an integrated view of their customers' buying behaviours, support needs, and uses of telecom.

Chapter 11: Utilities

Overview

Time is running out for utilities to make the move to customer-retail focused organizations and remain in control of their core product. It will take years to hire the talent, implement the new customer-focused technologies and change their organization's business processes to reflect the new demands and requirements of the customer-retail model.

As utility companies try to move from asset-based business plans to customer-based business plans, they are identifying the ability to retain the most profitable customers as their key objective.

For the customer, this means better presented services and more options than pay up or be cut off. For those utilities that get it right, fast enough, the opportunity is to move from a mature, low growth sector to a new high growth one.

They will face stiff competition from supermarkets — already some non-utility customer focused players such as supermarkets are entering the energy markets in the more deregulated markets of New Zealand and Australia — as are other organizations with large, well serviced customer bases. And to survive they will need to adopt the sophisticated technologies and marketing know-how employed to such good effect by national retail chains.

How utilities will change

As any consumer-focused organization knows the name of the game is customer retention. The key to success is to keep the profitable customers by providing exceptional customer service combined with flexibility in payment, billing and service options. The services that customers are coming to expect and the amount and types of customer information that the utilities will need to meet those expectations will be the keys for success in a customer-driven environment.

So what does this mean for the electricity and gas utilities that have been in their present form for the past 100 years?

First, the typical engineering, asset management focused mentality now prevalent at almost all utility organizations around the world will only be with us for a few more years — a decade at most. The next generation of utilities companies will not only offer electricity, gas, telephony, but also financial services, banking and an almost limitless number of products and services.

The company from which customers buy their utility products and services will be from any number of industries that have a large customer base and large amounts of quality marketing data on those customers.

The utility organizations that choose the customer-retail model will have the opportunity to go from a mature industry with almost no growth to one of growth, increasing profits and expanding employment. Such success will require coping with extreme competition and an ability to be flexible and innovative in providing products and services, responding instantly to each individual customer.

The key to success is to keep the profitable customers by providing exceptional customer service combined with flexibility in payment, billing and service options

As incumbent electric utilities gear up to face a deregulated retail marketplace, many have focused their efforts on cutting costs — downsizing their operations and negotiating new contracts with power generators. These efforts, while necessary, will not be enough to create enduring competitive advantage.

The greatest opportunity for far-sighted managers to create real value for customers and stockholders is a in the domain of retail pricing. A company must be able to move from regulated rates based on costs to market-driven prices based on customer value.

This shift will require an improved capacity to gather customer — and competitor — information relevant to market-based pricing. It will also require the acquisition of new pricing tools and the ability to use those tools quickly to make and implement sales and marketing decisions. It will also require a change in the conceptualization of the customer relationship, which is no longer a bilateral relationship between supplier and customer but a triangle that includes the competition.

The challenge

The current wave of deregulation will result in customers having a choice as to who provides their utility services, the level of service they want and the prices they will pay.

The key driver for customers when choosing their utility providers is price — a very close second will be high quality service which will be judged through all the interactions the customer has with the organization through all of the possible business channels. Deregulation marks the end of the traditional model of monopoly utilities with attitudes towards their customers as merely meters that consume their product and are sent a bill with the only options of payment or being cut off.

This in turn is causing competition which is leading to a customer-retail revolution and an immediate need for the utilities to adjust or develop strategies to retain their existing customer base and in particular the customer segment that is the most profitable.

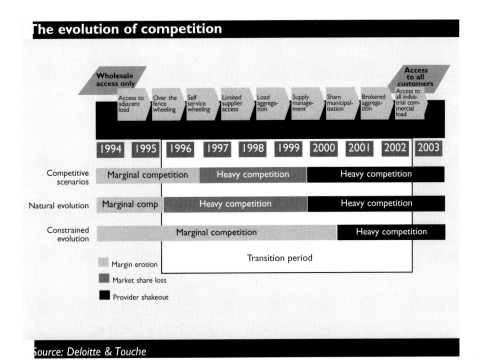

The evolution of competition

Source: Deloitte & Touche

How competition will develop

Deregulation is causing the utility sector to split into two organizational groups. One is asset focused, characterized by commoditization, regulated longer-term returns, decreasing employment and consolidation of the number of utility companies, and increasingly more competition from independent power producers and merchant plants.

This is the group of utilities that is currently focused on expanding their operations by buying assets outside of their traditional monopoly territories, in many cases on an international scale. They have recognized that only by reaching huge economies of scale with seven million to 10 million customers will they be able to survive with the small margins being allowed by the marketplace.

Within five to 10 years there will only be a handful of these multinational utility companies operating in each region of the world and world-wide only a few dozen that will grow large enough to be sustainable. This is contrasted with the thousands of utility companies that exist today.

The other group is customer-retail focused, characterized by high quality customer service, high levels of competition and tight margins, multiple sales channels with bundled and value-added products, a focus on customer retention, and many new market entrants. This customer-centric model will also experience customer churn of 20% to 30% per year resulting from the customers' new freedom of choice.

In many ways, this group will have many similarities to the deregulated telephone sector with hundreds or even thousands of new companies being created along with the incumbents. The incumbents, however, will for the most part be newcomers to the world of customers and retail. For the companies that pursue this strategy and understand the benefits and value of the new customer technologies the rewards will be rich. This group will increasingly recruit marketing and IT professionals to deploy powerful customer technologies that will become the most significant skill within their core competencies.

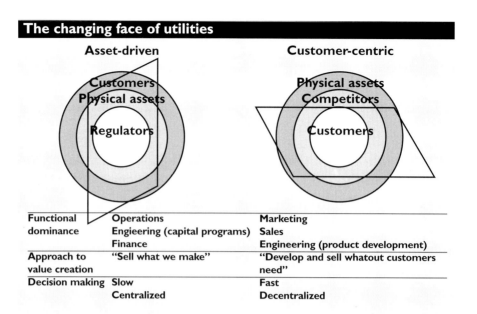

	Asset-driven	Customer-centric
Functional dominance	Operations Engieering (capital programs) Finance	Marketing Sales Engineering (product development)
Approach to value creation	"Sell what we make"	"Develop and sell whatout customers need"
Decision making	Slow Centralized	Fast Decentralized

Source: Deloitte & Touche

While the customer-retail group is certainly the area of greatest opportunity, it is also one where the traditional utilities will experience many hurdles that they are not designed to cope with. The more obvious include the ability to handle the many new entrants that will be offering huge price discounts combined with a variety of innovative products (some might say gimmicks) to acquire customers and an ability to quickly respond to the marketplace.

They will do this through powerful customer information systems, databases and related technologies that will allow them to make instantaneous decisions as to the desirability and profitability, both now and in the future, of the potential customers.

The technology and how to apply it

The shift from the asset-driven organization to the customer-retail driven organization will require changes across all aspects of the company, including its people, business processes and technologies.

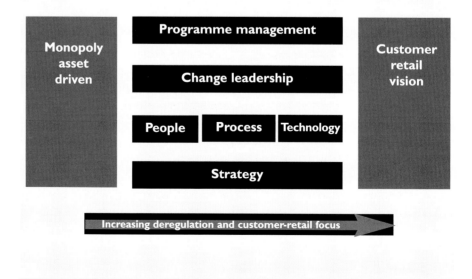

Source: Deloitte & Touche

While each of these aspects are important, it is generally the people issues and the way in which a company goes about the change management process that will be the key factor in the success or failure of any new initiative to a customer-retail focused utility. This is especially true in utilities whose employees are making the shift from monopoly status to competitive and deregulated status; in many cases becoming a private company at the same time.

People

In the customer-focused utility, the employees with the most contact with customers will be the customer service representatives (CSRs). Regardless of how good the price or product offering is, it is the interaction with the CSR or field sales group that will become the primary vehicle for selling those services and they will be the main influencer on customers and their image of the utility. This is regardless of how much effort and money is spent on brand development or marketing campaigns to get a customer to call.

The CSRs and field sales representatives will need extensive and on-going training on the technology they will use and products being offered. They will also need to have some authority to make decisions on the spot to keep customers from churning while they are interacting with the customer.

Consistency and quality of service is also critical for both utility staff and third-party representatives in the case of outsourced services such as system maintenance. It will require re-training for existing employees to make them familiar with the new customer-retail focused culture and a commitment from new and outsource providers that they will provide the service that the customer-focused utility has contractually agreed to provide its customers.

These are areas that can be controlled through the setting of appropriate benchmarks, customer satisfaction monitoring and compensation incentives, all of which can be enabled by customer-oriented technologies.

Customer technologies allow management to see more clearly what is happening across the whole organization and how retail strategies are, or are not, being met. It therefore becomes much easier (and necessary) in this environment to consolidate the management function to one decision-maker across all the divisions that have customer interaction. This shift for existing utilities will be by far the most difficult transformation they will face due to resistance to change that come from the various departmental managers.

Processes

For incumbent utilities the transformation to a customer-retail focus requires a change in the business processes currently in place, particularly for existing call centres and other areas of customer interaction. Instead of the customer information systems revolving around the needs of the utility's asset managers and back office functions, they must now shift to focus on the customer.

More importantly, customer information systems must identify those customers that are providing the largest profits. These customers must be treated with personalized, one-to-one service to keep them from switching to a competitor. Other customers will require high levels of service as well; however, they should be serviced through automated systems to as great an extent as possible, to reduce the cost of providing them with service. The work involved in developing the processes for both the one-on-one high value customer and the automation of the processes to cope with the other customers are underestimated at the utility's peril.

A degree of flexibility will be required to meet customer needs in the customer-retail utility, particularly as customers receive offers from other utility retailers. If the incumbent is lucky, their customers will contact them to see if it will at least meet the offer from a competitor.

More than likely though the incumbent must design a process to identify those profitable customers who are at risk of churning and begin a process of communicating with them to meet their needs. Flexibility will also have to be designed into the processes to take account of the variety of sales and marketing channels that will be available to the customers — not to mention things like payment and billing options that customers will come to demand and expect.

Technology

Technology for customer-retail utilities will see major changes to their customer information systems, call centres and field sales and marketing. Most significantly, in most utilities these systems are currently customized (one-off systems designed specifically for a particular utility). These systems are prone to large maintenance costs, large numbers of IT systems experts required to operate and maintain them and huge costs involved in upgrading due to the amount of reprogramming that must occur.

There are now software package providers offering off-the-shelf solutions that can be easily tailored to a specific utility's needs. Some software organizations have developed packages that are specifically designed to meet the needs and requirements of a customer-focused utility in a deregulated environment.

Critically, the new customer technologies for the utility sector must be capable of being integrated into the back office systems. In a utility this could mean the accounting and billing systems are automatically notified when a customer contacts a CSR to start a new service or some similar incident.

Regardless of which channel the customer uses to interact with the utility, it should always appear as the same to them. Meanwhile, the utility employees must see the customer in the same general manner, each with access to the same information as all the others, where regulatory restrictions allow.

Business users

In the commercial and industrial customer segments, particularly the largest of these customers, the utility market is ideally suited to using sales force automation systems. Instantaneous understanding of who are the key members of the client's organization, the historical background of the relationship and issues that have arisen, as well as access in the field to all electricity pricing trends, will prove to be invaluable tools for the key account managers.

Because most commercial customers already have smart meters which allow them to monitor their energy consumption patterns for periods as short as every 15 minutes, they will be able to use this information to bid for the lowest energy costs from energy retailers. Giving a field sales representative the ability to access that information real-time while at the client's site will help them provide better service to the client.

Domestic market

In the domestic market (individual homes and apartments), call centres will continue the trend towards greater voice automated response systems, defaulting to a live person only when the customers have complex enquiries, or they get fed-up with the listening to the computer.

When they do get through to a real person, all the details of that customer will appear on the CSR's screen and the first question the CSR will ask is "How can we help you today Mrs Smith?" And once the query is handled, the customer information system may prompt the CSR to ask Mrs Smith if the problem that she called about — for instance last Tuesday — had been resolved to her satisfaction. This will be possible, even though Mrs Smith probably spoke with a completely different CSR, or maybe the problem had been an issue that came up when a service crew was at her home, and she had never called anyone at the utility.

The collection of consumption information in the domestic market is the most expensive retail activity for utilities with each bill sent to a customer costing between $2 and $20 per mailing. As smart meters become commonplace the cost of collecting the consumption data will be reduced to inconsequential levels as the data can be reported electronically and automatically transmitted back to the utility or even directly to an outsourced billing house.

Even e-commerce has become a viable way for customers to buy and subsequently pay for utility services with this trend expecting to increase dramatically over the next several years. The whole billing process could even become mute as smart meters capable of using pre-paid energy cards — as used for public phones today — become more popular.

These technology trends will have a big impact on the processes and people issues that a utility or energy sales organization must consider for success.

The opportunity

Because most utilities come from a background of vertical integration, with generation, transmission and distribution, and retail operations all in one organization, deregulation is forcing them to unbundle this arrangement and treat each of these functions as a separate business unit or to sell them off entirely.

The result is that utilities will have to decide which of these functions they will focus on and then make their product offering attractive enough to retain their customers and update or install customer information systems that support the new customer focus for that part of the utility industry.

At the retail end this also means that previous barriers to entry such as access to huge amounts of investment capital for infrastructure have disappeared. An industry that in the past would require a minimum of several hundreds of millions of dollars to become a player will now only require as little as a million or two. This relatively meagre amount of capital will buy the latest customer information systems, marketing and branding budgets and a skeleton staff of professionals to negotiate the supply and service contracts with third-party service providers such as call centres.

The result will be potentially large numbers of nimble newcomers that will compete against the known utilities in a fierce fight for customers.

In this brave new world of deregulated customer-retail focused utilities, many traditional utility companies are finding their existing customer information systems, billing systems, call centres, pricing models and product offers are woefully inadequate for what customers and the marketplace are demanding and what potential competitors are already offering.

They will need to move fast to replace existing systems, many of which are custom-made and running on software that is 20 to 30 years old. Software vendors are able to offer off-the-shelf software packages that have many advantages over customized systems, not the least of which include the incorporation of best-practices along with relatively simple ways to tailor the packages to the unique attributes of their users.

Utilities will also need to become expert in sales and marketing as well as learning how to profile customers to identify those that may be in danger of churning or which will be likely candidates for the latest product and service offerings. To get it right, however, will be more complicated than it first appears and the skills that most utilities already have in sales and marketing departments are not likely to serve them well in a deregulated and competitive environment.

To make matters even worse, recent customer behaviour suggest customers will judge the service provided not just against other utility providers but against all the organizations from which they interact with — regardless of the industry or product they offer. This is raising the bar for service expected from utilities to the level of those organizations that are already known, either locally or globally, for their high levels of service.

A utility customer information system in this new deregulated customer-retail focused environment is characterized by being capable of:

- integration with logistics and financials;
- business process-oriented user interface;
- adaptability to any company structure;
- universal billing engine able to handle all types of contracts and products;
- customer orientated instead of asset or billing orientated;
- supporting both front office and back office organizations;
- handling new smart meter technologies;
- operating in an open architecture to communicate with third-party systems;
- object-oriented business approach; and,
- Internet enabled.

Putting this in perspective, the following table depicts the characteristics and skills that a call centre and its customer service representative that are found in most existing utilities and those that are needed a deregulated customer centric one. It is critical to remember that the nature of characteristics found in the current monopoly utility models must still be offered in the deregulated

Changing characteristics of call centres

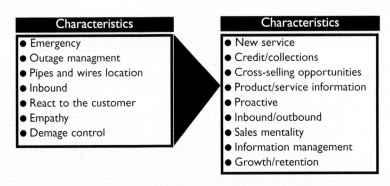

Characteristics	Characteristics
• Emergency	• New service
• Outage managment	• Credit/collections
• Pipes and wires location	• Cross-selling opportunities
• Inbound	• Product/service information
• React to the customer	• Proactive
• Empathy	• Inbound/outbound
• Demage control	• Sales mentality
	• Information management
	• Growth/retention

Does not require two separate call centres, but does require different enabling technology and skill sets

Source: Deloitte & Touche

environment, however, new skills, business processes and technologies are needed as well.

The future

The greatest area of contention within the utility sector is what the industry will look like in five years and beyond. It is highly probable that competitive, customer-retail focused utilities offering multiple products with core competencies based around customer service and marketing-based information technologies will be the major utility players.

The product mix for the customer-retail oriented utility providing products and services will look something like this.

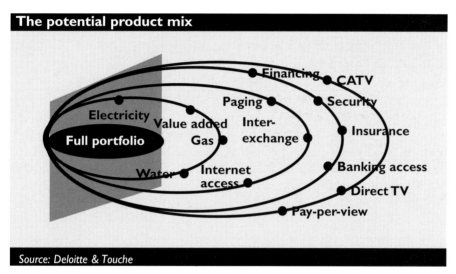

The potential product mix

Source: Deloitte & Touche

Bundled services and products combined with excellent customer service and deep expertise in retail business will be the trademarks of the customer-retail utility model. However, it is not certain that the utility company of old will still be the service provider of tomorrow. Those utility organizations that are prepared for the customer-retail focused model — as opposed to waiting to see what will happen (as most are doing now) — are likely to be the shakers and movers in the future.

For those utilities that move first into a true customer-retail multi-utility model, the initial investments in customer technologies may be difficult to justify in the short run. The cost of not doing so, however, will lead to a marginalization of the utility and quite possibly its destruction. Utilities must see the investment as just that — a tool for revenue and profit enhancement, not one of simply cost reduction.

Chapter 12: Making it happen

Overview

Buying the vision is not enough. There is no shortage of companies that recognize the need to turn their technology-focused and asset-driven organizations into customer-focused organizations. But when they implement the new systems, the benefits in the initial business plan are not there. Sales have not risen nor market share increased. The number of highly profitable customers remains flat. So what have they done wrong?

The root of the problem is often that although the organization has been redesigned along customer-facing lines, the design of the call centre has been left to the technicians and equipment vendors. They delivered a state-of-the-art system on-time and on-budget, but what was really needed was a set of people and processes supported by technology that would support customers where and when they needed it.

In today's competitive market, with product differentiation through good design and innovation becoming harder to achieve and impossible to sustain, the provision of outstanding customer support now lies at the heart of competitive strategy.

But making that strategy work means resolving questions that set the parameters for how the vision is implemented. So how should one approach the design of a customer support system? How does one carry out a design that never loses its focus on the customer and that only calls in the experts when needed? How does management design and implement its vision without analysis paralysis, without entrusting both vision and business to the IT department?

Although many companies do not plan the support function at all, expecting the right size of organization to grow up around their needs as they happen, this introduces them to high risks that can be avoided. Better is for the service organization to evolve as the product is being developed, and the product to be developed with support in mind from the first conceptions of the designer to the moment when it is in the hands of millions.

Implementing the change: internal and external

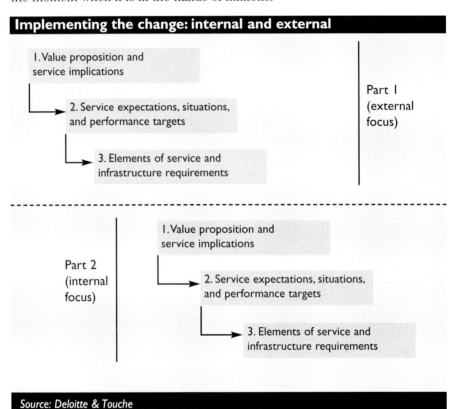

1. Value proposition and service implications

2. Service expectations, situations, and performance targets

3. Elements of service and infrastructure requirements

Part 1 (external focus)

Part 2 (internal focus)

1. Value proposition and service implications

2. Service expectations, situations, and performance targets

3. Elements of service and infrastructure requirements

Source: Deloitte & Touche

Planning framework

Step 1: Define the customer value proposition

A value proposition usually consists of a set of statements that encapsulate the customer's profile, their expectations, the design of the product and the environment within which the product will be used — and most importantly, how the product will fulfil the customer's needs. These values should each be sufficient to make a customer say they will buy the product.

To define the value proposition one needs to understand the intended customer well. The marketing department will have spent time identifying the customer as part of any product development and launch and should know a great deal about the intended customer's lifestyle, spending patterns, aspirations and the like.

This understanding of the customer should not be thrown away as soon as one starts to look at how they are going to be supported. The fact that there may be several distinct customer types and several value propositions must be borne in mind — for example a computer may be targeted at both domestic and commercial consumers which have two different sets of values.

As soon as the value proposition has been agreed upon, the next step is to look at how it will drive the services offered. For example, if part of the value proposition is that the product is a portable device on which a business person will rely completely for contact names and addresses (say, an electronic organizer), a number of service drivers can be extrapolated: integrity of the address database; reliability of the device; need for help from any location at any time. These facts will drive service — product support may be needed in the office and also the home, at any time of the day — but it is probable that expected response times need to be faster in the office than at home.

Once these are decided the required response is worked out — if the customer is going to use the device 18 hours a day, support will be needed during that time. If they are likely to use it in several different time zones, this must be extended to 24 hours.

Once these drivers and customer expectations have been identified a picture of the key service requirements can be put together. This can get confusing, so it may be useful to cluster these requirements under generic headings — one set is:

- **Channels and response**: the channels through which the customer will contact the service organization and what sort of response they expect;
- **Key competencies**: the capabilities of the service organization; and,
- **Information and administration**: this includes such topics as what the customer needs to be told, and what levels of advice and billing.

The clustering and generic headings will vary between products and value propositions, so it is best to define the set of requirements first.

> After having categorized what the customer needs, the next step is to look at the response that must be made to these needs and categorize responses for them

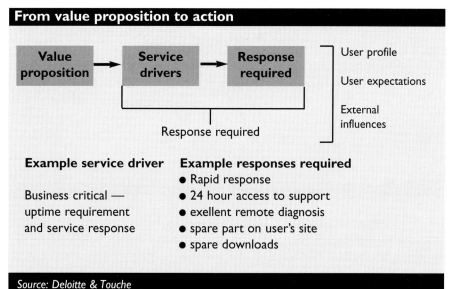

From value proposition to action

Example service driver

Business critical —
uptime requirement
and service response

Example responses required
- Rapid response
- 24 hour access to support
- exellent remote diagnosis
- spare part on user's site
- spare downloads

Source: Deloitte & Touche

Step 2: Understanding customer needs

Much of the work to date will have been done inside the organization using brainstorming, interviewing of knowledgeable company people, generic market research, even hearsay. It is now time to look more closely at the customer, their needs, and practical solutions to these needs.

A first step in discovering these support needs is to create a set of user situations where support may be needed. This is best done using sample groups of people that fit the customer profile, and a mock-up of the product. As well as helping the development of the product itself, a set of scenarios will allow possible problems to be identified and the response to them defined.

In defining these it is useful to start with the customer using the product for the first time. For most consumer electronics products 40% of support calls are made in the first month of ownership, according to the 2:2:1 rule — being two calls the first month, two the rest of the first year and one thereafter.

These initial responses are usually at the level of "can't switch it on" or "can't make it work". The causes can be multiple and may be difficult to define. However, these needs will be met with straightforward answers as long as the causes are fully identified and the support organization prepared to respond to them.

The next group of situations will be centred around the day-to-day use of the product — say, "I can't use it abroad" — which will be more varied with more complex solutions. The final group will be more esoteric and come from the more expert user wanting to know, perhaps, system compatibility requirements.

When a comprehensive set of situations has been worked through with an accompanying list of possible causes of problems, the next need is to identify a set of support requirements or elements of service and the performance considerations that must be applied to each element of service.

For example, if the cause of a support need is that the device is physically broken, the support requirement will be for information and processes to be available for registering repair and for dropping off and collecting the product. The elements of service will be instructions on the packaging, helpdesk information and the physical repair pipeline. The performance considerations are such items as proximity of drop-off points, response times of collection and delivery services or availability of helpline staff.

Categories of support — the response

Assistance with using the device

Obtaining product information

Problem diagnosis and resolution

User

Obtaining software updates/accessories

Fault repair (service engineer)

Sales

Administration

Source: Deloitte & Touche

After having categorized what the customer needs, the next step is to look at the response that must be made to these needs and categorize responses for them. For example, if the user does not know how to use a device, the response

Categories of support — the demand

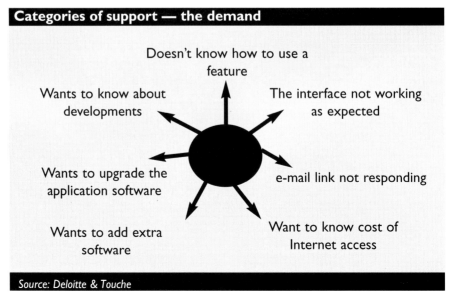

Doesn't know how to use a feature

Wants to know about developments

The interface not working as expected

Wants to upgrade the application software

e-mail link not responding

Wants to add extra software

Want to know cost of Internet access

Source: Deloitte & Touche

will be "give assistance in using it". If the user needs to upgrade software, the response is to provide upgrades. At this stage the means or channels of response do not need to be defined — but one needs to be clear about the nature of response that must be made.

Step 3: Define the response

Once one has some understanding of the response required, one should be in a position to say in which ways one should support or keep in contact with the customers and agree the foundations of the infrastructure needed.

The elements of service required need to be defined. Briefly, it is a component of the overall service provision. It typically includes some combination of trained human resource, materials, procedures and systems. It is designed to address one or more specific causes why the user is not able to use a particular product or service satisfactorily, and consequently needs support.

Some examples of it are: sales literature, user instructions; account management and billing; and on-line help and diagnostics.

Again, to achieve a full set one must form clusters based on the causes of support needs and the responses defined earlier in collaboration with the sample set of customers and assumptions as to what the customers will do and need.

A complete set of service elements should then allow one to outline the support infrastructure. This is the basic structure showing the number of levels probably needed, the relationship between the customer and service, the main channels of communication, and the relationships within the company between service, R&D, repair centres, internal services and external organizations.

Infrastructure for consumer support

As one builds up the infrastructure, the service elements which will be addressed against each element should be checked. For example, the on-device help in the diagram below may include user instructions, interactive help, and on-device diagnostics. One must also outline the key competencies and the information needed to support people and processes within each part of the organization.

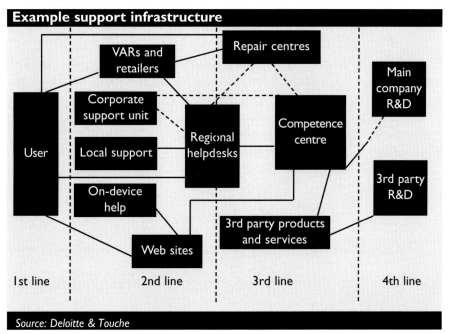

Example support infrastructure

Source: Deloitte & Touche

Step 4: Preparation, planning the organization and infrastructure

Organization

One now needs to be clear about the attributes, competencies and values of the staff, and the principles and rules that need to be set down to ensure the service mission, vision, values and operating principles of one's organization are clear.

The first step is to investigate the implications the value proposition will have on the internal aspects of the service organization. Close consideration of the value proposition, best done by current members of the service organization unless the new product is expected to bring about radically new support requirements, will generate a set of implications.

For example, if the value proposition states that the product will be sold to the domestic and corporate markets, then: the organization must be prepared to talk to corporate and domestic customers, and the policy on charging for support must be clear (domestic customers expect free support during the guarantee period, corporates may wish to pay for enhanced service).

A quick "sense check" will probably be needed to test if the implications are practical and supportable. But if they are, a mission statement should be constructed directly from the value proposition. Links between the two should be direct and complete. For example, if the value proposition states that "the product is designed for mobile business people to communicate throughout western Europe at any time", then the mission must state that the service organization "will support business users in their own language throughout western Europe 24 hours a day."

As soon as the mission is clear, one must ensure that the values implied by the mission are built into the organization and that their implications are made clear, otherwise it may be ignored. Rather the values that the mission implies and requires should be extracted if it is to be realized.

Unfortunately, values stated on their own tend to sound glib — "professionalism, quality, integrity..." are essential to all organizations whatever their purpose.

So a pertinent set of values should be defined and then the implications these values will have on the organization. So if a value is "quality", the implication in the organization may be that "activities must conform to quality standards which must be measurable and measured. The organization should be perceived as a quality organization by its corporate and domestic customers."

If this is all pulled together — the service mission, the elements of service, the values and the infrastructure requirements — the company then has a vision of its future support organization.

The final step before defining the support infrastructure in detail is to derive the operating principles for the support organization. This should be a simple list driven by the agreed vision and values which will help the organization to define how the vision will be realized and shape the construction and staffing of the infrastructure.

Examples of operating principles are:

- single point of contact;
- best practice call handling;
- discretion in dealing with business information;
- use of performance measures to assist continuous improvement in call handling; and, say,
- continuity in customer interactions.

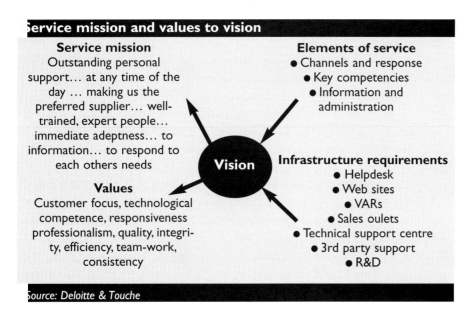

Service mission and values to vision

Service mission
Outstanding personal support... at any time of the day ... making us the preferred supplier... well-trained, expert people... immediate adeptness... to information... to respond to each others needs

Values
Customer focus, technological competence, responsiveness professionalism, quality, integrity, efficiency, team-work, consistency

Vision

Elements of service
- Channels and response
- Key competencies
- Information and administration

Infrastructure requirements
- Helpdesk
- Web sites
- VARs
- Sales oulets
- Technical support centre
- 3rd party support
- R&D

Source: Deloitte & Touche

Infrastructure

The next step is to tie things together. The example below shows the links between the vision, the service mission, the company's values, the elements of service and the part of the support infrastructure that must respond.

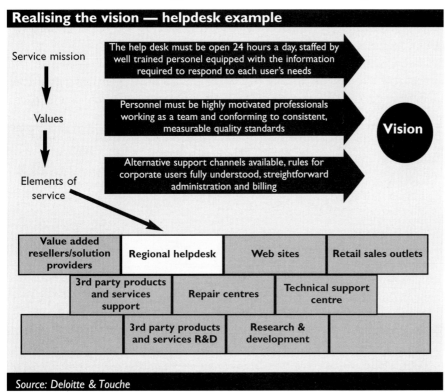

Realising the vision — helpdesk example

Service mission

The help desk must be open 24 hours a day, staffed by well trained personel equipped with the information required to respond to each user's needs

Values

Personnel must be highly motivated professionals working as a team and conforming to consistent, measurable quality standards

Elements of service

Alternative support channels available, rules for corporate users fully understood, streightforward administration and billing

Vision

Value added resellers/solution providers	Regional helpdesk	Web sites	Retail sales outlets
3rd party products and services support	Repair centres	Technical support centre	
3rd party products and services R&D	Research & development	

Source: Deloitte & Touche

For each element of the foundations one must define:
- Role. In simple terms, what the element provides;
- Functions. A list of the activities performed;
- Infrastructure. The systems and physical infrastructure needed for people to do their jobs within the element and within the overall structure;
- Organization. An outline of the organization structure and terms of reference for the different functions performed by people within each element;
- Dependencies and key linkages. The main links with other parts of the organization, the main information needs and the support it needs to perform its functions and develop; and,
- Performance measure. How the element as a whole and key functions within

will be measured to ensure continual improvement and notification in changes in performance

To predict the scale of the support required, one must consult the design, production and marketing parts of the company. If a product is under development, design should already be discussing how much support should be built into the product, production should ensure that there are no endemic faults that may swamp support, and marketing or production should decide on the box or other written instructions, sales and dealer product training, and overall launch plans.

To determine the scale of the support organization, one must work closely with the marketing organization to link the scaling up of the support organization with the roll-out of the product. Product plans should inform as to when and in which countries the product will be launched, and how many products will be in use in each market during each, monthly or quarterly, period.

One then has to build up a model of the number and type of problems customers will encounter, and the number and nature (according to category of support) of calls that will be received from customers, the number of products that will be returned for repair, and by inference the number of support positions that will be needed month by month.

The model will be influenced by:

● projected number of products in each geographic market by period;
● likely types of call (for example, simple FAQ versus complex technical);
● expected number of support requests per customer;
● anticipated role of support people (for example, support only or support + sales + administration); and,
● probable distribution of calls (for example, the pattern for support of business applications is that needs fall away on Friday afternoons);

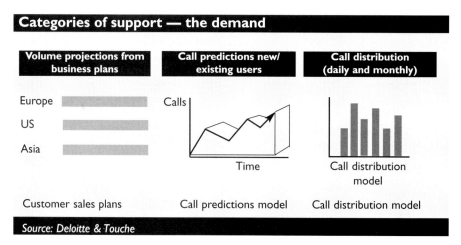

Categories of support — the demand

Volume projections from business plans	Call predictions new/ existing users	Call distribution (daily and monthly)
Europe US Asia	Calls Time	Call distribution model
Customer sales plans	Call predictions model	Call distribution model

Source: Deloitte & Touche

This model will determine the number of support positions that will be required and when they should be filled.

The overall result is a model, based on investigation, theory and practice. However, it contains many uncertainties — are the sales predictions, assumptions on user call numbers call types right? What if the product never breaks down (mobile phones are far more reliable than at first assumed). Or is there an endemic fault that will swamp a sophisticated support organization?

Many organizations consider these constraints so great that they do not plan the support organization at all, expecting the right size of organization to grow up around needs as they happen.

However, this introduces them to high risks that can be avoided if the model is developed alongside the product so that it is ready to receive the customer's support needs as soon as the product is launched. To do this the service organization must evolve as the product is developed, and the product must be developed with support in mind from the first conception of a designer to a product in millions of customers' hands.

Step 5: Implementation

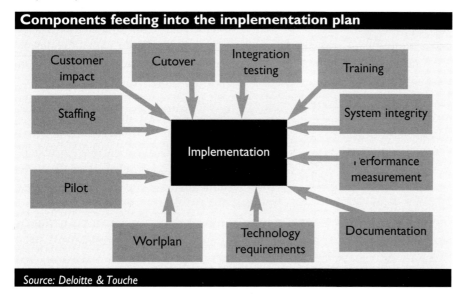

A call or service centre cannot be built overnight, and a large number of elements have to be considered and built into a well controlled implementation plan.

Work plan
An implementation plan will have multiple strands and involve people with different skills and needs on many different tasks. Key to the success of the implementation is a plan that ensures the right people are matched to tasks; that risks have been assessed and thought given to their mitigation; that contingencies have been built in; dependencies understood; tasks understood and agreed.

Staffing and training
One should have already identified staffing needs at the design stage. However, recruitment and training people takes time. As a general rule one should allow at least two months between job advert and person on the payroll; anything from a week to several months to train people in the products, their support, and the technology they will be using. If setting up a service centre in a foreign country, local customs and employment law need to be understood when working out staffing and training plans. Plenty of time should be given for all these activities.

Technology requirements
The technologies discussed in other chapters of this book may require expert help and the selection process for such assistance almost always takes longer than expected. Technical assessment, tendering, waiting for responses and selection is time consuming. This time must be built into the workplan. Technology requirements must consider functions, quality and risk.

System integrity
As well as bolting together the hardware and configuring the software to support processes, the performance and integrity of the system must also be considered. No customer wants to hear "the system's down" and so performance criteria must be stated at the design stage and traffic load predicted and tested as

part of the development. The integrity of transactions and data must be guaranteed — especially if confidential information is being held.

Integration testing

The end product will consist of a number of elements joined together by interfaces, processes, procedures and people. The integration of all these elements must be tested — with the full realization that testing cannot predict every eventuality. Tools and approaches for testing software are fairly comprehensive and are usually professionally used by IT people. The areas that are usually missed out are people and procedures.

Documentation

Nowadays documentation means more than paper. Media includes electronic text files, databases supporting case based reasoning tools frequently asked question (FAQ) databases; CD-Rom presentations and interactive demonstrations of products and product features.

The web is becoming a means of distribution of helptext as well as upgrades, bug fixes and additional features for products containing complex software. All this documentation must be managed to ensure consistency and avoid confusing the customer. Development, distribution and version control of all these documents must be built into the plan.

Pilot and cut over

No matter how well planned an implementation, risk will always be present and the unexpected will always crop up. To mitigate this, implementation should be phased if at all possible. Phasing can take several general shapes, governed by product/product group; location site/country/region; customer group/type. A general rule is to test if the technology works, offer all services at one pilot site, to see if the approach works, and try supporting one product or customer group from several locations.

If one is moving to a new approach and system from an old one, one must make sure the cut over is as smooth as possible. Surprises can be kept to a minimum by:

- getting the timing right;
- migrating data effectively — by working out what data needs to be migrated and planning well ahead; and,
- communicating — internally within the organization, externally to the sales channels and customers

Customer impact

It is vital that that customers' needs are borne in mind both during and after the implementation phase. The system, procedures and staff must be checked to stay in line with the value proposition, and, also, that that proposition is still realistic (for example, is the leading edge product still leading edge, is it still a premium product?). Occasional checks should be made on the market and any changes fed back to the project steering body for consideration.

Biographies

Lawrence Hutter (right)

Over the past 20 years Lawrence has worked with leading consumer products, consumer services and retailing organizations on a wide variety of strategic business improvement initiatives in the UK, across Europe and internationally. His business expertise lies in relationship marketing, account management, channel development, customer service provision and end-to-end supply chain integration.

He also has a strong track record in the successful application of technology as a key business enabler in each of these areas. Lawrence is a partner in Deloitte & Touche Consulting Group's global consumer business practice based in London. He started his career with Andersen Consulting and, in 1989, founded the specialist relationship marketing consultancy company Customers Limited which recently became part of Deloitte Consulting.

Ian Pattison (below)

Ian Pattison is a director in the consumer business industry practice of Deloitte Consulting. He has 20 years' consulting experience with consumer and industrial products companies in the areas of supply chain, customer service and marketing. His work has ranged from definition of strategy and business process change, through to detailed analysis, implementation and support. Thanks to an IT background he specializes in supporting business processes through current and newer technologies.

Neville Howard (below)

Neville Howard is a senior manager in Deloitte Consulting's London office, where he leads the UK's call centre practice. Neville has spent over 20 years in the telecommunications industry and now focuses on helping financial institutions and retailers exploit network technology. Neville led the editorial team that produced a sister publication, Deloitte Consulting's *The Network Value Proposition*.

Louise Brett

Louise is a senior manager in the Deloitte's financial services industry practice where she leads the sales process transformation services. Louise has spent 17 years in the retail financial services industry and focuses on the customer-facing aspects of the business, particularly around the effective deployment and integration of delivery channels and the enabling technology.

Paul Jackson (above)

Paul Jackson is a senior consultant specializing in realizing the potential of new media technologies, especially electronic commerce, the Internet/intranet and other innovative delivery channels. He also helps clients to develop and realize the benefits of a knowledge management strategy.

Paul has particular expertise in future business positioning/creation and business planning for new media technologies, having co-created and sold TIPs (technology investment planning services) methodology to a number of clients.

Paul has worked with a variety of clients including government agencies, FMCG organizations, charities, major retail banks, pharmaceuticals companies and utility companies. Consultancy projects have included new product/service research, knowledge management strategies, developing Internet/intranet strategies, implementation planning and creating a vision of how innovative IT usage can provide strategic advantage.

Lisa Neal-Graves

Lisa Neal-Graves has over 13 years' experience in telecommunications and is a senior manager in Deloitte's New York customer dynamics practice. She offers a blend of technical/engineering expertise and market management experience in the areas of product research and development, marketing, and management of telecommunications systems and services.

Before joining Deloitte & Touche Consulting Group, Lisa worked with Lucent Technologies, US West and AT&T Bell Laboratories. She led the launch of the first full feature Internet-based call centre solution among telecommunica-

tions network equipment providers for Lucent, earning the 1997 Call Center Product of the Year award from *Call Center Magazine*. She has extensive experience in implementing IVR, AIN, and reengineered technology infrastructures.

She earned her ME in Engineering Management from the University of Colorado at Boulder, her MS in Computer Science from Michigan State University, and her BS in Computer Science/Mathematics from Hampton University.

Tom Porter

Tom Porter is a manager in the Deloitte Consulting e-business group. He has 11 years' experience working in both systems and consulting and helps clients address the commercial and technical issues around e-business.

Paul Beddie (below)

Paul Beddie is a manager in Deloitte Consulting's Asia-Pacific energy practice and is working out of the Sydney, Australia office. Since joining Deloitte Consulting, Paul has participated in energy projects in the Asia-Pacific region focusing on the creation of virtual retail sales and marketing organizations and IT enabled reengineering of internal service organizations.

Before joining Deloitte Consulting, Paul had eight years experience' in marketing and sales, including over five years in the global business development division for power generation projects with a major Japanese engineering and construction firm based in Tokyo.

Paul graduated from the University of Colorado at Boulder with a BA in International Affairs and recently attended the Stanford University-NUS executive programme.

Vimi Grewal

Vimi Grewal is a manager in Deloitte's London office. She joined the firm in 1998. She has many years of consulting experience across multiple industries focusing on the design and implementation of major call centres covering all functional areas of an organization.

She has recently been responsible for the management of customer service improvement plans. This has included the reengineering of management processes and the implementation of an enhanced knowledge based decision support management system for a large entertainment organization and the implementation of customer service initiatives for a number of financial institutions.

A graduate in Computer Science & Information Technology from London Guildhall University, her areas of specialty are financial services and the customer dynamics/enterprise service management service lines.

Anthony Ruback (below)

Anthony Ruback is a manager in the consumer business industry practice of Deloitte Consulting. He has taken a lead role in developing category growth strategies for market-leading FMCG manufacturers, focusing on optimizing range, merchandising and promotional strategies. He has led a number of projects for UK and European grocery retailers, developing and implementing new processes for buying, merchandising and category management. Before moving into consultancy Anthony worked in FMCG marketing management.

Barbara Deskey (above)

Barbara Deskey is a senior manager with Deloitte & Touche Consulting Group in Atlanta. She is a leader of the firm's initiative to drive comprehensive transformation of customer-facing activities (marketing, sales, customer service and order fulfillment) in the telecommunications and media industry, from customer-focused strategy and processes to implementation of enabling technologies and organizational management practices.

Her clients include AT&T, Cox Communications, Bank of America, Bell Mobility, BellSouth Telecommunications, BellSouth Cellular, MCI, Nortel, US Cellular, and the World Bank.

Before joining Deloitte & Touche Consulting Group in 1990, Barbara served as a product manager for cellular and wireless applications for AT&T Federal Systems, and as an internal consultant and assistant controller for Morgan Stanley & Co. She earned her MBA with distinction from the Wharton School (University of Pennsylvania) and her BA with honours from Duke University.

Ramon Tisaire

Ramon Tisaire is a senior manager with Deloitte Consulting in Chicago. He focuses on customer dynamics specializing in business process redesign and implementing leading-edge technologies. He has helped many international organizations transform their sales behaviours such as Gruma in Mexico, Groupe Schneider in France and Telecom Italia.

He is currently on a two-year assignment in Deloitte's Madrid office as part of the firm's global career development programme. In his new role, he is serving as the European operations manager for customer dynamics, while contributing to the development of the service line in Iberia.

Biographies

Sue Desai (above)

Sue Desai is a manager in Deloitte Consulting's public sector industry practice in the US. She has over 10 years' experience providing organizational, operational, and information technology consulting services to federal, state, and local government agencies, as well as major financial and high-tech firms.

Her experience includes process analysis and reengineering, organizational analysis and design, change leadership, training, programme management, risk management, systems development and integration, and international business development.

Rory McLaughlin

Rory McLaughlin is a partner with Deloitte Consulting's public sector practice. He has over 20 years' experience in the planning, design, development and implementation of financial and special-purpose information systems.

Rory serves as Deloitte Consulting's practice leader for the public sector employment industry information technology group in the Americas, where he focuses on providing public sector clients with leading edge technology solutions. During his career, Rory has implemented systems that support state government agencies administering labour, human resources, transportation, retirement systems, education, child protective services, and revenue programmes.

Kate Amos (below)

Kate Amos is a senior consultant in Deloitte Consulting's reengineering for results practice. She has an MBA from the Cranfield School of Management, where she focused on marketing, service operations strategy and process, developing a strong interest in customer-focused processes.

She has nine years' consulting experience in operational research, IT implementation and reengineering, gained in FMCG manufacturing, utilities and public sector organizations.

Chris Battersby (below)

Chris Battersby is a manager in Deloitte Consulting's reengineering practice. His background is in large international systems development projects in the consumer products arena. Over the past couple of years he has concentrated on developing and implementing customer-focused approaches to business change that consider people rather than technology as the driving force for change.